GOD DON'T MAKE NO JUNK

Peggy MacTaggart

THEYTUS BOOKS

MacTaggart, Peggy, 1942-

God don't make no junk / Peggy MacTaggart.

ISBN 978-1-926886-12-1

1. MacTaggart, Peggy, 1942-. 2. Métis women--Biography.

I. Title.

FC109.1.M33A3 2012   971.004'970092   C2012-903023-6

Book design by Ann Doyon

Printed in Canada

THEYTUS BOOKS

www.theytus.com

In Canada: Theytus Books, Green Mountain Rd., Lot 45, RR#2, Site 50, Comp. 8
Penticton, British Columbia. V2A 6J7, Tel. 250-493-7181
In the USA: Theytus Books, P.O. Box 2890, Oroville, Washington, 98844

 Canadian Patrimoine
Heritage canadien
We acknowledge the financial support of The Government of Canada through the
Department of Canadian heritage for our publishing activities.

 Canada Council Conseil des Arts
for the Arts du Canada

We acknowledge the support of the Canada Council for the Arts, which last year
invested $154 million to bring the arts to Canadians throughout the country. Nous
remercions le Conseil des arts du Canada de son soutien. L'an dernier, le Conseil a
investi 154 millions de dollars pour mettre de l'art dans la vie des Canadiennes et
des Canadiens de tout le pays.

 BRITISH COLUMBIA
ARTS COUNCIL

We acknowledge the support of the Province of British Columbia through the
British Columbia Arts Council

GOD DON'T MAKE NO JUNK

Contents

Dedication

I dedicate this book to my parents.
I honour the difficult path you took upon yourselves
in guiding and supporting me.

I thank you from the bottom of my heart.
I dedicate this book to my precious children
who gave me the honour of being their mother and
who taught me many lessons.

I dedicate this book to my wonderful grandchildren
who enabled me to see life through the eyes of
innocence.
I dedicate this book to a special old gentleman who,
with his tough-love approach, encouraged me on the
good path of life.

I dedicate this book to a respectful and loving young
man who,
with his patience and kindness, was able to support
me through reliving the pain of growing and who,
with his sense of humour, guided me to laughter and
letting go.

Acknowledgements

These truths are written for the Creator and all the Spirits whose voices I am now listening to.

Thank you, Creator, for letting me be known as Angekwe, the White Wolf Woman who Flies with the Eagles.

Thank you, Creator, for the many Elders and Medicine People who have walked with me through my own personal hell and who gave me the medicines I needed to heal myself and to take my rightful place in life.

Thank you, Creator, for my loving parents, who continued loving me when all others would have abandoned me as I walked my journey of destruction, and who continued to support and guide me when I turned my life around to pursue the Red Path.

Thank you, Greg Sommerville, for giving me the encouragement I needed to put my story down on paper. Without your teaching and helping me to write, this book never would have been written.

Thank you, Canada Council for the Arts, for believing in me and for sponsoring my trip to the Banff Aboriginal Writers course in 2007, the workshop that started me on my writer's journey.

Authors Note

I am a sixty-nine-year-old Ojibwa-Scottish grandmother, looking back on her life with both humour and sadness combined with some hate, anger and resentment, ultimately feeling serene and spiritual with a very strong connection to the Creator. This is my own story; the events in this book are true. Out of consideration for my family, I have changed the names of all of the people and many of the identifying details.

The story begins with a young girl, Bobbi's, childhood in Northern Ontario. While her father is overseas in World War II, she receives powerful teachings from her Ojibwa grandfather. Later, she rejects the Red Path after being subjected to physical, sexual and emotional abuse. The story shows how people experience many levels of hell, when in pain and various methods of disassociation.

This book confronts childhood sexual abuse and what it was like for a Métis child dealing with horrific traumas as well as an alcoholic parent. The story explores alcoholism, abuse, marriage breakdown, divorce, life as an Aboriginal single parent, descent into alcoholism and drug addiction, and eventual recovery. The full circle becomes complete in the story, when Bobbi gets sober and clean, returns to her roots, follows the Elders and Medicine People, and becomes whole again. When the Elders and Medicine People deem her ready, they send her on her journey of sharing and helping others open the door to their own healing—which, in turn, continues her own inner healing.

The target audience of this novel is mainly young Aboriginal people who feel lost and unloved, and who may feel that they have no apparent direction in their lives. In reading my story, they will hopefully realize that if this Kokum (grandmother) can find her way home, anyone can. What I would like to say to you is this: Everything is going to be all right. Believe me. I know. I do not say this just because I am optimistic. I know the drill on controlling one's destiny—I have all the tapes and CDs. I'm not blind either, figuratively speaking. I do not say that everything is going to be all right because of some planetary-alignment zodiac science thing, although I love all that stuff. No. I know this because I'm here, alive, well and at peace, except for this cough from smoking too many cigarettes.

Today, many look upon me as an Elder and some even see me as a Medicine Woman because of my work with people. What I really am is a regular old grannie, proud as punch of my children and grandchildren, including the many young people that I have met throughout the years who look upon me as their mom or grandma. I am usually in good humour but certainly know how to get 'madder than hell.' Fortunately, I have been given the gift of always finding something funny about life events.

By telling this story, I am hoping to help you on this bewildering and confusing journey called life. Bobbi's story is going to be hard to read but it also shares many beautiful experiences and happy times with a wry sense of humour. I have learned that balance in all things is what life is all about. Without pain, it would be impossible to appreciate the wonderful experiences in our lives, because there would be nothing to compare them to. I'm telling you this story as an experience that I hope will shed some light on your life somehow.

Whenever I feel confused about what to do about a current situation, I put on my moccasins and walk out the front door to my one-legged brother, the great birch tree that stands close by. I offer him tobacco for being there for me and I put my arms around him and hold him, listening to his sighs. Everything is going to be all right. I know, because *God Don't Make No Junk.*

Peggy MacTaggart

Prologue

A few nights ago, a terrible howling animal sound woke me up. Looking out the window, I saw a man in the driveway and he appeared to be hurting an animal. I couldn't tell for sure because he had his back to me, but somehow I got the idea he was hurting my cat Satellite. Still groggy, I threw on my moccasins and crept outside to catch him in the act. He was wearing a leather jacket and a baseball cap and he had a blond ponytail hanging out the back. He looked about five foot nine, about a hundred and sixty-five pounds, likely around forty years old. Sneaking up to him from behind, I grabbed him by the ponytail and threw him to the ground with the drive and aggression of a wrestler. I almost scared the poor guy to death.

It turned out he was just letting his dog do his business in the bush off of my driveway and wasn't hurting my cat at all. The guy called me all kinds of names, even though I apologized like crazy. He accused me of being a maniac. He wasn't hurt or anything, except for his ego I guess, lying down in a muddy puddle. I almost laughed. But I realized that he could get violent, so I said to him, as innocently and sweetly as possible, "My goodness, my dear man, if you think I am a maniac, you should come into the house and meet my six-foot-two husband. As a matter of fact, I would gladly make you a coffee."

He stood up quickly, shook himself off, grabbed his dog and, with his head down, took off as fast as his feet could carry him. I guess he figured getting body-slammed by a grandmother doesn't exactly give you bragging rights. I don't actually have a husband and for that matter I live alone, but I certainly didn't want him to know that.

Let me describe myself to you. My name is Bobbi Priestson and I'm sixty-nine years old. I'm wearing an old t-shirt that has a drawing of a white wolf standing on a mountaintop, howling at the moon. There's a tea stain on it and I don't care. I am wearing blue jogging pants—also stained. I have twenty-three teeth left to my name, unless I wear my dentures. My hair is still a caramel brown and I wear it long, but it's usually all messed up, unless I'm going somewhere special like a restaurant with somebody. I wouldn't want to embarrass my dates looking as though I were on welfare—which I'm not, though I wouldn't feel bad if I were.

On the wall behind my computer desk, which is peppered with cigarette ashes, hangs an eagle feather, which I rightfully earned on my path with the Elders. In case you haven't figured it out by now, I'm Indian. Ojibwa. Well, half. The other half is Scottish and much of my early life revolved around being half and never complete. People consider mixed bloods like me, Métis.

In my younger days, I was five feet four inches and a hundred and five pounds of pure sweetness, wrapped in a soft vanilla wrap of a woman. I had breasts like Florida oranges, legs like a river of gold and a face like an angel. I was that beautiful young woman with a sword in her hand, standing tall, head up and eyes fearless, filled with anger and ready to fight.

On the inside, however, picture this: a toddler being picked up by its torso and lifted to shoulder height and then slammed into the walls of a dark, muggy, cold cave. Picture the child crashing into the rock wall, and hear it cry a loud shriek and fall to the ground. Hear the sad cries of that child and that was me on the inside for a very long time. Now visualize the cave door closed shut.

You would never have seen that. You would have just seen me playing the part of the strong, belligerent woman. But I was hurt and I was angry. I was so angry at the world for how things went. I was quick to blame others and feel sorry for myself, finding argument after argument to justify all of my anger. It never occurred to me until much, much later to even think of forgiving some of the people who hurt and abused me. It never occurred to me to take accountability for any of my own, often atrocious, actions towards others. To be honest I almost destroyed myself the first thirty years of my life because I harboured such destructive attitudes, which I maintained by feeding them daily. I had so many resentments eddying through my veins that I was misery and pain incarnate.

Before returning to the Red Path later in life, I lived a life full of self-pity. I was self-centred. Everything had to go my way. I was all important and grandiose as though I were my own God, as though I controlled everything. Somehow though, when times were tough and I found myself alone on my bed, coiled up and sad, through all the eerie silence of the house, I believed there was a Creator outside of me. How else could nature develop as it did, I wondered, if it weren't for Kitchi-Manitou the Great Spirit, who took care of everything from ants to grizzly bears? I believed, however, that Kitchi-Manitou had turned His back on me. He didn't want to look at the vulgar mistake He had regretfully created.

My negative and self-destructive way of living did not come about from a total lack of moral direction. Meshomis, my Ojibwa grandfather, said many wise and helpful things when I was a little tyke. During hard times, I could sometimes hear him whispering in my ear, 'Hey, my little darlin', remember to thank the Creator for your tears, 'cause they will clean your eyes and you'll see things in a different way.'

Meshomis warned me many times about the Black Path. Unfortunately, later in life, I wrote off these beautiful lessons as an old man's ramblings. When abuse, neglect and alcoholism invaded my life, his lessons seemed to disappear for a time, while I rebelled against the evil that I was exposed to. It was only many years later that I returned to the Red Path of the Medicine Wheel, the Aboriginal way of following God's will as opposed to constantly fighting the inevitable and insisting on your way. Fortunately, Meshomis lived to see me begin to pay attention to his teachings and to begin to follow the Red Path to the best of my ability, before his journey to the Spirit World in 1975.

Unlike what you see in the movies, Meshomis's voice and traditional teachings did not appear before me, later in life, as a vision to tell me to stay on the Red Path. It wasn't as though I was sitting at a bar doing bad things when all of a sudden his voice echoed in my head, leading me to get sober and get my life together.

My life became full of neglect, abuse, drugs and alcohol, and for a long time it was easier to be the victim. The teachings of Meshomis only came back to me when the difficult journey to healing had already begun.

Chapter One

From my first moments of being able to understand and react to anything, I was worried about God's attitude towards me. I was positive that the Creator wasn't a half-breed and I was extremely sure that He wouldn't want such mistakes ever returning to live with him. I felt doomed. That terrible word 'half-breed' was imprinted on my brain at a very tender age. I grew up believing I wasn't a whole person, that I was a mistake. Children as well as adults know how to be cruel.

"Hey, half-breed, get outta here," the Reserve Indian kids would yell. "You don't belong with us. You're just a wannabe Indian. You're really a white spy and we don't want you near us. Go home. You're a mistake."

If I didn't run home they would throw mud balls at me. The white kids were just as bad as they yelled all kinds of filth at me. I wondered why nobody accepted me. I had long brown hair, dark eyes and pale skin. I was slender and very pretty. There didn't seem to be any outward reason for such rejection from both races.

"You're nothing but a horrible little savage that's going straight to hell when you die," the kids would yell at me. "While you're alive, you are just garbage and you're going to grow up to be a hooker and a drunk. You don't belong anywhere. You're just junk. Even God doesn't want you."

I knew that I didn't have a chance in hell of making any progress with God. Fortunately, I loved my Indian grandfather, Meshomis, with all my heart and soul and most definitely preferred to listen to and believe his teachings of life. It seemed those teachings were in complete contrast to those of the white man's God.

During the first few years of my life I spent a lot of time with Meshomis, in Northern Ontario. Meshomis said many wise things to me when I was a little tyke. He taught me about the ways of the Creator of All Things. I thank the Creator every day for my Indian grandfather. I learned about respect and consideration through teachings of nature. I learned the importance of always being honest and humble. I now understand the experiential way was much easier for a child to grasp than biblical studies.

Meshomis was able to instill a small seed of integrity within me that flourished no matter how much I tried to silence it. Later in my life, I dismissed Meshomis's teachings because I made myself believe for a time that they came from a man living in a dream world. Even though Meshomis guided me in the Indian way, it was he who first encouraged me to 'pass as white.' On the other hand, my white grandparents, who were upper middle class and the furthest thing removed from being racist, told me to be proud of my Indian heritage. All this resulted in more inner confusion. I never knew which family was right and which was wrong. It seemed like there were two ways of life, and I liked both of them. Many years later, I realized that Meshomis was trying to protect me from all the abuse he had suffered as a young Indian kid in the early 1900s. Because I had my father's white skin tone, he felt I would avoid being bullied if I passed as white.

Remembering exactly how Meshomis looked and being able to visualize this extraordinary man as if he were standing beside me enables me to describe him and some of his teachings. No, he did not have long black braids hanging to his waist. Nor did he wear a headband; nor was he six feet tall. He was an ordinary looking man who wore his black hair cut short on the top and sides but with some length on the back, parted on the left side of his head. Quite often, when he bent his head, his hair would fall over his eyes and sort of perch on his rather large nose. He stood five foot nine inches tall with quite a slight frame. His face had a chiseled look, which could be somewhat intimidating. I was devoted to him and willing to listen to him by the hour. The moment he looked at me with his almond-shaped black eyes, I tended to pay attention to whatever he said, instinctively knowing whether I was going to receive a lesson or a lecture simply by his tone of voice.

I could tell I was his favourite, because he would call me over, "Hey, little twerp, let's go for a walk 'cause we need to talk." Many Indian grandparents called their favourite grandchildren 'twerp' as a pet name, so I really felt honoured. I made sure my cousins were aware I was the favourite.

He had a gentleness and softness that shone from his eyes whenever he looked at me, although I have seen those very same eyes become extremely severe. Sometimes, when he felt the need to protect his own, they appeared to me like dark coals in the snow. His style of dress usually remained unchanged. He wore dark blue polyester pants with a blue flannel plaid shirt, or a green flannel plaid shirt with brown polyester pants. Around his neck he wore a long leather cord holding his Sacred Medicine Pouch. The only time he took off his Ojibwa patterned moccasins was to replace them with heavy Indian boots in the winter. When he performed ceremonies, he would change his flannel shirt to a ribbon shirt and put on his headband.

One beautiful fall morning, Meshomis took me in his birchbark canoe to show me where the wild rice grew. It was important to learn about wild rice and the harvesting techniques because it was a food staple of the Ojibwa Indian tribes of Northern Ontario. On our way to the designated area, we had to portage past some rapids in the river. Before continuing our voyage, Meshomis asked me to look at the rapids and to see and feel their strength.

After a few minutes, he said, "Angekwe," which was my Indian name, "never forget that you are one drop of water. Alone, you are nothing. You are powerful when you reach out to others for help and when you reach to others to help them. You must be honest and always know that all living things are made from Kitchi-Manitou, the Creator of All. It is not you who created any living thing. He even gives you the power to choose which direction you are going to travel. How will you follow the rapids? Will you be aggressive or will you be assertive? How do you see these rapids?"

Meshomis was a great man. He was a great teacher, but I had no answer for him. At the time, I had no clue what he meant, but

I liked watching the river flow. It was soothing. The answers to his questions came to me slowly and inconsistently, sometimes years later.

Another fine sunny day, he found me raiding the garden breaking open the pods and eating the fresh green peas.

"Hey, little twerp!" he called. "Do you want to come with me down by the lake? I got some things you might want to see."

What a silly question. I would have gone anywhere with him at any time. He always had a fantastic story to tell and I wondered what the teaching would be this time.

"Sure thing, Meshomis, I am ready now," I answered gleefully. I happily skipped alongside of him trying to keep up with his long strides. Once we got to Eagle Lake, which was less than a half mile away from the house, I sat at the lake's edge while Meshomis took some tobacco out of his deerhide Medicine Pouch. He placed some tobacco by a tall maple tree and said a few words in Ojibwa too quietly for me to understand. I often wondered what the tobacco ceremony was about because he did the same thing every time he taught me something. When the ceremony ended, he returned to me and we sat together on the sandy beach. He had a long twig that he had picked up by the tree. He drew a circle in the sand with one horizontal line and one vertical line crossing each other in the middle. Then he planted the twig in the middle where the two lines crossed.

"This is a Tree of Life," he said. "The Indian people look at life as a Medicine Wheel. Life is a circle. What goes around the Wheel comes around the other side. There is a purpose and a teaching attached to every event in our life."

I had a whole lot of questions but I knew not to ask because whenever I did, he always replied, "You will know when it is time for you to know."

He sat silently by the circle. He took out his Sacred Pipe and began to smoke it.

Finally, my curiosity prevailed. "Meshomis, please give me some 'bacco, I want to feed the real tree like you did."

He let out his big belly laugh and answered me joyously, "You finally figured it out, huh, kiddo? Doing things is more important than asking questions. Come with me and I will show you what I do at the tree."

We went over to the tree and he showed me the little mound of tobacco at its base and explained that when he has something to teach, he offers tobacco with his prayer and asks Kitchi-Manitou, the Great Spirit, to give him the right words to use. Then we went back to the circle in the sand.

"Angekwe," he spoke seriously, "I want you to pretend that this tree is you. The Creator is there in the tree too because He is everywhere but you can't see Him. Do you understand what I mean?"

"I think so, Meshomis. The Creator is with me wherever I am. You and Mommy always say that the Creator is always with us and that the trees were our one-legged brothers."

"You got it, kiddo. Aren't you just the smartest little girl I know?" He continued, "This line represents the Red Path and the other line represents the Black Path and the whole circle plus these two paths are known as the Medicine Wheel. When we choose the Black Path, we are choosing the opposite of what the Creator knows is good for us. We stop growing. We do things that are bad for us. When we forget the Creator, it's as though we are left in a cold dark cave all by ourselves.

"Meshomis, I don't understand you," I told him.

"Angekwe, when you came to this world as a little baby, the Creator gave you what we grown-ups call freedom of choice. This means that you can do things that are good for you and for other people, or you can do bad things and get yourself in trouble and hurt yourself and other people. It's all up to you to choose which path you are going to walk. We call the good one the Red Path. The other one is the Black Path. It's normal to fall on the Black Path once in a while, Angekwe, because we are only human. But we can hurry back and get on the Red Path again where the Creator wants us to be."

"Oh, Meshomis, I'm scared because I do bad things lots of times. How do I get back on the Red Path?" I asked, hoping it wasn't too late.

"Well, sweetheart, you have already started. You just admitted that you have done bad things. That's a big step. Another thing you can do is to ask people you upset to forgive you," he added more seriously.

I suddenly thought of what I had been doing in the garden. "Meshomis, I need to go and tell Gran I was stealing her peas. I need to do that right away and I won't even care if she spanks me or yells at me. After that, I'm going to be real careful not to be bad anymore. I'm going to make everyone proud of me."

A wide grin spread across his face as he ruffled my hair and said, "Go for it, kiddo."

One day after the rain had stopped and a fantastic rainbow had appeared on the horizon, I ran looking for Meshomis hoping that he would teach me about rainbows. I found him sitting and fishing off an old log that was perched on the side of the creek. He always sat so quietly, so serenely, as though nothing ever bothered him. He was hooking a worm on his line as I appeared from the woods. Meshomis noticed me and motioned for me to come and sit by him. I hoped I was going to hear one of his stories, told only the way an old Indian gentleman could, but I sensed it wasn't going to be about rainbows. This time it was a powerful example of the Black Path.

"Angekwe," he began, "which path did you decide to walk today?"

I told him I hadn't really made a decision. He smiled.

"Many moons ago," he began, in his storytelling voice, "a little worm was born to parents who named her Ookashahgumme-kwe. They loved her dearly and wanted to dote on her, but they did not know how because they were orphans who had had a difficult life and had to fend for themselves growing up, never learning how to show love, having nobody to teach them. Her parents fed her very healthy green leaves every day. That is what worms are supposed to eat because it makes them healthy. Do you know what I mean, twerp?"

"Yes, Meshomis, just like me when Mom says I have to eat my greens if I want to grow up to be big and strong."

"That's right," he affirmed. "But Ookashahgumme-kwe was not happy. She did not like being a worm: 'I hate being a worm. Look at me! I'm good for nothing. All I am good for is to be food for the birds or the fish. I hate myself!' She felt very alone and she thought her parents didn't love her because she never felt loved.

"So one day, while Ookashahgumme-kwe was crawling around

and crying, she met a mosquito. 'Hey! Ookashahgumme-kwe!' said the mosquito. 'How would you like to be the strongest worm in the land? All you need to do is eat these live maggots and you will be.'"

Meshomis continued, "Because she was very needy and wanted to be the centre of attention and she figured she wasn't loved as much as she thought she should be, Ookashahgumme-kwe decided to become the most powerful fat-bellied creature on the land to gain control over everything around her. And so she took to eating the live maggots the mosquito offered her.

"The maggots did make her powerful and strong. She could fight spiders and win by curling up around them like a boa constrictor. But they also made her insanely bitter, angry and hateful. She felt no love for anything and only said cruel things. She refused to eat the green leaves her parents would give her because she thought they would make her vulnerable and weak and she did not want to be sad ever again.

"Finally she became rude, impolite and aggressive to everyone around her, including her parents. Her parents eventually asked her to leave their home because of her destructive nature, which made Ookashahgumme-kwe even more defiant.

"She wiggled across the earth continuing to eat only maggots until she grew ten times in size and until she was as big as a garter snake. Her belly was full of living maggots and she became the biggest worm in the land and she fought many insects, killing and devouring them. One day she found herself at the edge of Lake Superior and decided that she was strong enough to defeat what lay in the lake as well. In she went and swam out to where the fish lived.

"She looked at the fish condescendingly and sneered, 'I am Ookashahgumme-kwe and whereas you are ugly and weak I am very strong and powerful.' A small fish swam over to her, looked at her and answered, 'You are very powerful indeed, Ookashahgumme-kwe'—and promptly lunged at her and ate her. Poor Ookashahgumme-kwe never learned about the power of love, understanding and compassion. She never learned to give but only learned to take. Her selfishness killed her."

"Yikes, Meshomis," I started to cry. "You're being mean to me and scaring me. You know that I can't be a good little girl all the time. I don't want to get full of maggots and I don't want to be eaten up by a little fish."

Meshomis gathered my shaking little body into his arms and whispered softly, "Don't worry, honey, that won't happen to you because your Spirit that lives inside of you is powerful and wants to know only good. Yes, you will sometimes go off the right path but you will always find your way back to the good one."

The first three years of my life were spent near Migisi Sahgaigen, where I lived with Mom, Meshomis, Gran, Uncle Wendall, Aunt Marie and my cousins David, Lola and Wayne. This picturesque area of Northern Ontario had many beautiful tourist camps, where tourists came from all over North America to go hunting and fishing and stay in log cabins. These camps were immersed in the natural beauty of the forests and waters, which existed in great splendour and peace. I enjoyed looking out on the lake, watching the ripples of water and hearing the splash as they gently touched the land. I watched a mother duck keeping her babies all in a row as she kept a careful eye out for bald eagles that were looking for a fantastic meal. It was an ideal life for a child, experiencing nature in its glory. The waves splashed upon the shore as though asking us to go for a swim, the trees waved hello as the wind gently caused them to sway, and fluffy clouds danced across the sky.

I loved everything about living in the bush with my family. There was so much to see and so little time to do it. My aunts and uncles used to say, especially when they were drinking, that I stuck as close to my Indian grandfather as shit sticks to a blanket. I felt like I had to hog Meshomis's time because I knew I would eventually be moving away with my parents to a city somewhere, once my dad came back from the war. There were many bears, wolves and moose that lived close to us with their families. Mom didn't allow me to go too close to the animals but I enjoyed watching them play in the woods. I made friends with the partridges and the squirrels. But my most noteworthy befriending was Little Red.

Little Red was an honest to God real-life fox. When I first saw him, he was limping and dragging his right hind leg. For whatever reason, he came around our house every day at ten-thirty in the morning, but he seemed to be getting weaker by the day. Meshomis said that he was weak because he couldn't hunt for food anymore because of his injured foot.

"How would you like to help this little fox, Angekwe?" Meshomis asked.

He awaited my response with anticipation. He always made me feel like my opinions were of utmost importance to him, but this time I was far too excited to have an opinion of any sort.

"What do I do? What do I do?" I was bouncing up and down and frantically pulling at his shirt. I was excited as all get-out to help Little Red.

"Here," Meshomis handed me our dog dish. "Take Frisky's dish here and fill it with dog food. Then go and put it between the woods and the house where you can see it. This way, Little Red will be able to eat right here and you can watch him!"

'What a great idea,' I thought. Meshomis sure was smart. And kind, too: he was always going out of his way to help animals. There was no such thing as brand name dog food back in 1945; at any rate, we sure didn't own any.

What Meshomis meant was to fill the food bowl with table scraps. So I did. I also filled a large basin with rainwater from the barrel we kept behind our home. I placed the food and water about a hundred feet from the house, but made sure that I could keep an eye on the events from the kitchen window where I glued myself for the morning, making sure I didn't miss a thing.

Sure enough Little Red arrived on our property at just around ten-thirty. He tentatively approached the food I had laid out and ate it. I was so happy and excited I wanted to scream for Meshomis to come and see the show, but I knew better not to scare the small red creature. Then, for some reason, Little Red leaped into the water basin and rolled around in it until he had given himself a bath!

Then, when he finished splashing and twisting himself about in the water, he drank it! I was astounded. I thought it strange that Little Red drank the very water he washed himself in, but he seemed to know what he was doing and Meshomis had told me how smart foxes were. So far this dog food thing was working out pretty well, I thought.

My success encouraged me to continue with the same routine

until Little Red was better. At Meshomis's suggestion I moved the food and water closer to the house each day. Every morning I waited an eternity for the beautiful little animal. After a few days, I moved from my window watching post to the front porch to watch my new friend. Little Red hesitated when he saw me but I could see the beginnings of trust in his eyes even though he was skittish when he came for his scraps. He seemed so wise and wonderful.

His long red fur glistened in the rain, sparkled in the sun and even glowed in the mud.

Meshomis told me that Little Red would instinctively recognize my smell and therefore he would become more and more familiar with it, which would be a good thing. So, I made perfectly sure not to bathe anymore in order to be smelly every day. This became a priority! I got away with it for a couple of days too, but when Meshomis realized what I was up to, he went into gales of laughter, so much that he had to hold himself by his elbow over the kitchen counter when he saw me going around covered in dirt from the previous two days. I don't think he could have laughed any harder. Evidently, I had misunderstood Meshomis's teaching about the sense of smell in animals. Finally, ten days into my feeding routine, I put the food right beside me and Little Red came and got it. Mission accomplished.

I brought out some celery and carrot sticks to ply him with too. I gently took them out of their paper wrap and extended a celery stick out to him, almost touching his wet little black nose. He bit it out of my hand and worked on it off the porch trying to chew it, which he sort of half did. I then held out a carrot; he came and snatched it away from me and took to it like the celery but was only half successful with it. Long veggies are not a usual fox diet, I was to learn, so I imagine that Little Red was just being polite. He sure had good manners for a wild animal.

That was to be the last day I saw Little Red. But it didn't really matter to me because Meshomis had explained that the precious little fox needed to live with his own kind and for me to be grateful that the Creator had chosen me to help him in his hour of need. At that point, I made a vow to myself. I decided to help people and all living creatures whenever I could.

Chapter Two

Close by the small reserve where I lived was Lac LeVieux, where my cousin Edith lived with her mom and dad, my Aunt Myrtle and Uncle Stanley. I would visit back and forth between these places when I was young.

Although the leaves have turned their gorgeous reds, yellows and brilliant orange many times since I was a child, I can still vividly recall the differences between the Indian Reserve and Lac LeVieux. Lac LeVieux was a complete contrast to the Reserve, with its surrounding forest. Everything in Lac LeVieux was a dull grey, and the colours of nature could only be seen on the horizon. They may well have called it by its English translation 'The Old Lake' because of its barrenness and dreariness which gave you a feeling of being lost in a fog. There were no parks and the only grass around was in sunburned yellow patches. The smoke stacks that rose from the local dump slyly peeked over the distant hill and sent out the smell of rotted, burning garbage. It was an awful odour that could make you feel nauseous, especially on hot days.

Living by the dump was a sure sign of poverty, visibly noticeable by the coating of soot covering all the buildings in the vicinity, and by the lack of town facilities for young children to play in. The only play area was the gravel pit to the right of the dump, where you couldn't do much at all except chase and capture snakes. The pit swarmed with black and orange snakes, as well as bright green ones.

There were flies everywhere. They were in your food and in the coffee. If you were a drunk, like many of the male residents, you had flies in your beer. There were flies sucking on the inside of empty beer glasses, sucking the residue sugar and salty spit from the toothless, slobbery mouths of the residents of this horrible place. I have no good memories of this infested hole of a town, except for those of my cousin Edith, whom I dearly loved. Edith was my best friend. We were like Butch Cassidy and the Sundance Kid, except we were three-year-old girls. Instead of being full-grown train-robbers, pursued by a pack of unyielding lawmen, we were partners in the battle against drunken relatives. I watched over her and she watched over me.

Edith's home was at 376 Lilac Road. Her mom was my mother's sister, Myrtle. Her dad's name was Stanley but everyone called him Stinky because he was a fat, greasy barbarian who always stank. He reeked of sweat and stale booze and had pockmarks all over his unwashed face, and boils covered his grimy body. He was grotesque. Their home was as desolate and uninviting as the hellhole feel of the rest of the neighbourhood. Its roof was covered with water-stained, pea-green, ragged, unevenly laid, unfinished shingles, which matched the sunburned patches of grass.

Next to Edith's house was the Summit Hotel, which had gone into receivership some time ago. It was now abandoned and rotted and being used as a bootlegging station. It stood crookedly at the end of Lilac Road. The weathered wood of the hotel's exterior walls looked as though they had never been painted, varnished or cared for. Sitting on the steps of the hotel were several fly-ridden bums, whom the government didn't even know about. They hung around, avoiding the war and getting sloshed. Even I knew that most reputable men would have been fighting for their country in World War II at the time.

Despite the miry filth and rubble surrounding us, playtime with my cousin Edith was loads of fun. Instead of playing skip rope or having a tea party with a doll set, Edith and I used to play Chase Drunks with snakes. On a really good day, we could catch several snakes and hide them in a canvas potato sack, then carry them back from the dump in the little red wagon we shared. We could use the snakes as effective weapons for chasing the drunks out of Edith's house by sneaking in with our canvas sack and, when nobody was looking, dumping the snakes out on the floor. We would hide and joyfully watch all the drunks clumsily scatter out.

One Friday afternoon, Mom and I arrived for our visit and it was pouring rain. Aunt Myrtle was washing some dishes.

"Oh hi, Leona! Hi, Bobbi!" she called to us. Nobody called me Angekwe except Meshomis because the rest all pretended that our whole family wasn't Indian. They used to tell everyone that we were dark-skinned French Canadians.

Aunt Myrtle had her hair in a ponytail and she was wearing an old housedress and slippers. She looked tired. As soon as Mom and I sat down, Uncle Stinky pointed to me and Edith and yelled, "Don't think you two brats are staying in here to annoy us. Go outside and play right now."

Edith and I knew better than to argue with Stinky, especially when he was half cut. We stood on the porch in the pouring rain for a few minutes, becoming angrier and wetter by the moment. Edith finally stomped her foot and announced, "Let's go catch some snakes and sneak 'em in the house!"

I nodded in agreement and hurried to get our little red wagon while Edith got the potato sack from under the kitchen sink.

"I told you to get the fuck out of here!" Uncle Stinky yelled.

Off we went to the dump, two little waifs in the rain with not even a jacket on our backs. We arrived at the gravel pit and enthusiastically captured seven snakes—all of them bright green. Our strategy for capturing snakes was as follows: Edith took off running like a raving lunatic and snatched at a snake like a hyperactive dog fetching a bone and rammed it into the potato sack unmercifully, the snake twisting in vain in her small, fearless hands. I'd do pretty much the same thing.

On our way home, although soaked from the rain, we were delighted with ourselves.

"It'll be fun watching 'em get scared, eh?" Edith giggled gleefully. "Lots and lots of fun."

"Yeah." I smiled back at her, proud.

Unfortunately, our plan didn't unfold as we had hoped. Apparently we were gone for too long. As soon as he spotted us, Uncle Stinky ran out and grabbed Edith by an arm and a leg and hauled her into the house. Mom yanked me by the arm, spanked me and threw me into my assigned bed without supper. Edith dropped the potato sack when Uncle Stinky grabbed her. She snuck out later to retrieve it, although the snakes had escaped. She hid the potato sack under the kitchen sink again for future use.

On Sunday morning, Mom and I were awakened by a series of kabooms coming from the dump. Some teenagers were throwing in cans of aerosol, which exploded and were alarming the nearby crows who kept cawing to one another emphatically every time another kaboom sounded.

When Mom and I got to the kitchen, she was greeted by a bunch of drunken rowdy friends and relatives. Their welcoming smiles vanished from their faces when they realized Mom didn't have any booze, but the smiles returned when she produced the money for two cases of twenty-four. It was always the same. Everyone panicked until they were assured there would be enough beer. I looked around for Edith but couldn't find her between the drunken bodies scattered about the wood plank flooring.

As a rule of thumb, the hung-over drunks from Saturday nights would gather at Uncle Stinky's on Sundays because it was next door to the old Summit Hotel, the local bootlegging station. About a dozen were here this Sunday. Most of them were sprawled all over the filthy floor like uprooted trees after a hurricane. There was only one couch—brown and full of cigarette burns, which is why everyone was all over the floor. There was a cheap, wooden card table propped up precariously in the corner because it only had three legs—also brown. Its fourth leg was leaning, for aesthetic purposes I guess, against the corner where it should have been affixed. The small trunk that usually had its place in the opposite corner of the room was missing and I wondered where it was. The trunk would have normally been used for a table or seat.

Uncle Stinky was standing close to me. He always wore exactly the same thing: green workpants which were filthy, especially all over the backside, and a raggedy, long-sleeved, grease-stained shirt of the same green as the dirty pants. His sleeves were rolled up carefully to show off his muscular, blond, hairy forearms. He stood like a western gunslinger with his fat grimy thumbs tucked in his belt loops and his beer belly shamefully hanging out over his belt. His bottom shirt buttons couldn't be fastened because of his blubbery stomach. Underneath his shirt was a stained, holey yellow t-shirt. He also had on his beige steel-toed workboots that looked as though they wanted to kick you. The smell of him could make you queasy, like the burning garbage from the smoking dump. He had long, stringy blond hair that hung over his scarred face, which was peppered with pimples.

Aside from Stinky's uncultured appearance, he ended almost every sentence with the word bitch. "Get me a beer, bitch!" "Where's my supper, bitch?" "Shut those fucking kids up, bitch!"

On this particular day, he was wearing a gruesome smirk, revealing two rows of perfectly straight, yellow teeth, discoloured by his usual tobacco plug which he placed in his upper gums. He was presently chewing a wad, and the juice from his tobacco wad was dribbling over his bottom lip. He spit it out on to the floor. Splat. The room looked as though a dog that couldn't contain its bowels had crawled through the room. Between splats, Uncle Stinky made a big show of opening a bottle of beer with his teeth. He stuck an unopened beer between his upper and lower teeth and once he got a good grip on the cap, his face contorted and turned red and his facial veins pulsed out until he got the cap off. What a diplomat. He glanced over at me silently and took a long gulp from his beer. His eyes were glossy, faded blue and beady. I couldn't maintain eye contact with him.

Now what? I worried. I knew better than to ignore Stinky when he wanted my attention, so I made eye contact and tried to hide my fear. He kept chewing on his wad of tobacco, spewed another brown gob and wiped his chin.

George McLaughlin, who was sprawled over the brown couch, caught Stinky's attention. George was a friend of the family, I guess. What a great circle of winners my family's circle of friends was. He was holding a beer in one hand, which was hanging down at such an angle that beer was dripping slowly onto the crumby floor. Drool was running out of his mouth into his unkempt beard, then filtered to the floor in a long elastic drip. Dealing with George gave Stinky something new to do, so he left me alone for a while. He grabbed George by the beard and with a quick jerk of his wrist, managed to bring him to his uncoordinated feet, making him wobble like a newborn gazelle taking its first steps. Still holding George by the beard, Stinky pulled him to the door and threw him out.

"Fucking scum ball!" Stinky yelled, as George collapsed outside.

Stinky's logic dictated that it was okay for him to spit his brown phlegmy chewing-tobacco juice on the floor but not for George to dribble.

"Later, kid," Stinky threatened as he looked back at me.

My heart pounded with fear. I looked around to see if anyone had heard him, hoping that one of the ladies had taken notice of his words. No such luck. As in a bad dream, nothing seemed right. Most of the ladies had messed-up hair and loose bra straps hanging out of their wrinkled blouses. Everyone was laughing hysterically like insane clowns: loud, vile and out-of-place. I was puzzled as to whether they were having a good time, since they all looked so insane. Meanwhile, "Life is a Song" by Tony Bennett was playing, but when it finished nobody bothered to take the record off the phonograph, so its needle kept swirling back and forth, causing a loud, scratching noise. What a trashy place for any human being to be, much less Edith and me. All I wanted was to find Edith.

"Mom, please tell me where Edith is. I want to play with her. I promise we'll play quietly," I pleaded.

Aunt Myrtle informed Mom that Edith was in bed with a fever. Mom felt my forehead and decided that I should be in bed as well. She took me by the arm into what was referred to as the back bedroom, which in fact was just a bit larger than a walk-in closet. The walls and the ceiling had probably been painted white at one time but were now a dull grey. Edith was lying in a junior-sized bed on the right-hand side below a small, cracked, muddy window. On the left-hand side of the room was the trunk that was usually in the living room. It was a small, brown and yellow trunk that measured about two by four feet, just over two feet high. The top of the trunk had ridges. It was draped with a ratty, old blue blanket that was considered the mattress. There was a two-by-four leaning against the wall that resembled a wooden canoe paddle, similar to the one I used when canoeing with Meshomis. Edith and I were facing each other, separated by only a few feet of dusty, worn-out, wood plank flooring.

I noticed her arms were bruised, probably from the shoving and bullying she had received from Uncle Stinky the day before. She was so sick with a cold that she didn't bother to answer me when I asked her about the echoing booms from the dump, so I lay on my back on the mattress and rested.

A few moments later, someone snuck into the room, furtively checking back to see whether anyone had seen him come in, and softly closed the door. I knew it was Uncle Stinky by his stocky silhouette. He stood at the end of the trunk and leaned over me, balancing himself on his elbows, his ugly face just inches from mine. His sweat dripped down on my little face.

"You little bitch," he said in a terrifying tone that Edith could overhear. "You are going to lie perfectly still and you are going to let me do exactly what I want or I am going to take that fucking two-by-four and beat your little cousin with it!"

He made himself more comfortable, letting most of his weight fall on my arms, cutting the circulation. He looked as though he were going to do push-ups, which I had seen Meshomis do numerous times. Then he clamped his slobbery mouth over mine, almost covering my nose, cutting my capacity to breathe. His sweat continued to drip down on me from his fat, bloated, pus-peppered face. He then released some of his weight from my throbbing arms and pulled up my dress and pulled down my ruffled underpants. He unzipped his fly and pulled out his penis. The roughness of his hard hands and his jagged fingernails scratched at my legs as he roughly placed his penis between them, rubbing it back and forth trying, unsuccessfully, to penetrate me.

"C'mon, you little bitch," he repeated impatiently, as he pushed against my genitalia.

Incapable of entrance, he started to masturbate and he finished himself off all over my three-year-old body. There was this creamy stuff all over me.

The only thing that kept me from hollering for help through all this was that I had turned my head towards Edith and maintained eye contact with her while Uncle Stinky molested me. I could see the fear in her eyes and I wanted to reassure her with mine that we'd get through it and she wouldn't get beaten with the two-by-four.

When Stinky finished with me, he went over to Edith's bed and just sat there for a while. I was hoping he was going to give her a break but no such luck. He was just recuperating so he could attack her as well. She looked terribly sad as her father molested her. She kept looking at me, her eyes saying, 'This hurts, this isn't right, I want to die.'

I cried silently. When Uncle Stinky finished with Edith, he left as carefully and quietly as he had come in. That was that. When the party ended, Mom came to take me back to Aunt Marie's without the foggiest idea that anything was wrong.

The next morning when I woke up at Aunt Marie's, Mom was lying on the black, vinyl couch in the den with a wet facecloth on her forehead. She was wearing a white blouse adorned with little pink flowers, and it looked as though she should have smelled clean and fresh like baby powder. Instead, she stank of stale beer and cigarettes and her clothes were all messed up; her buttons were in the wrong buttonholes and the top three were undone. Her eyes were darker brown than usual and somewhat sunken into the back of her sockets. Her skin was yellow and sallow. I wondered how this change had come about so suddenly.

"Mom, Uncle Stinky hurt me," I started out.

"What did he do?" she asked disinterestedly.

"He got on top of me and was rubbing that big thing between my legs and he did it to Edith, too!" I forced out.

Mom stared at me, unable to believe what she had just heard.

"That's not true!" she yelled. "Your Uncle Stanley wouldn't do that to you. How dare do you say that? How dare you? You are a very, very bad girl to say such an awful thing about your uncle! You know it isn't true and I don't want you ever saying anything like that again to anyone! Do you understand me?"

"Okay, Mommy."

"Not ever! I don't want you ever to repeat that! Am I clear?"

"Yes."

Mom stopped taking me to Uncle Stinky's after that and we never spoke about the incident again, nor did I see Edith again for the rest of my childhood. I believed Mom when she said I was a bad girl. As for the memory of the event, I literally forgot the whole thing until I was well into my forties. I can't explain why. I guess it was easier for both Mom and me to go into denial rather than face the reality of what had happened.

For years and years after that day, as far as I knew, it had never happened. But even though I didn't remember the incident for years, I instinctively and subconsciously reacted to it. I started to think life would be easier if I just didn't care about others. I began to think that Ookashahgumme-kwe had the right idea. I figured if I could become strong and unfeeling like Ookashahgumme-kwe, nothing could hurt me anymore. So what if I got killed one day. It would be better than the life I had. I wished my daddy was around so he could take me in his arms and tell me that everything would be all right.

Chapter Three

Living in the bush on the Reserve with Mom's parents and other
family members was bliss, quite contrary to when she would take
me to her other relatives' places in Lac LeVieux for drunk-a-thons.
After all, in the bush I had Meshomis and all my cousins, and life was
an adventure for me. There were endless ways for me to keep busy,
especially around our little log cabin that Meshomis had built for his
family many years before my time. There were no nails in the entire
cabin. Each piece of wood had been carved to interlink with each
other.

When you entered through the only door you arrived in the
kitchen to the smell of bread baking in the oven and other goodies
cooking on the old black wood stove. Frisky, our old dog, usually
would be found snoozing under the stove on his old yellow blanket,
basking in the heat. To the left was a long table covered with a bright
red oilcloth surrounded by twelve wooden chairs which Meshomis had
deemed necessary to paint bright red. I had to sit extremely carefully
so as to not get my bottom pinched in the cracks of the seats.

To the right of the door was the living area consisting of a couple
of old but clean couches and an ancient radio perched on one of the
three small tables in the room. The other two tables held kerosene
lanterns. In the middle of the living room was a rickety and creaky
staircase that led up to the two bedrooms on the second floor. One
was for my grandparents who had a beautiful bedroom set with all
the appropriate trimmings, and the other one held three bunk beds
that Meshomis had made, thus enabling my cousins and me to sink
deeply into the feather mattresses and thick warm quilts that my

grandmother had made. Sometimes there would be extra cousins staying there while their parents were out drinking.

There was no bathroom in the house. Whenever nature called, we would wander to the outhouse where we could browse through an Eaton's catalogue as we attended to our personal needs. Meshomis had even put in a small window to let in light.

There was no electricity or plumbing, which meant that water had to be fetched. Fortunately, there was a spring close to the house so we had the purest water. There was always a lot of food. Meshomis had built a root cellar so Gran was able to keep all the vegetables she harvested from her large garden. He had also built a barn which housed a couple of cows, as well as a pony for our enjoyment. Meshomis also built a chicken coop where fifty chickens lived quite comfortably and, in return, gave us many eggs as well as their life when it was time.

One bright summer day, I had just finished my daily chore of feeding the chickens when I heard my mother's voice yelling to her father, "Meshomis!"

"What is it?" Meshomis asked, coming out from the back yard, where he had been chopping wood.

"Would you go and get a chicken, please?"

Supper ritual was about to begin. Normally, Meshomis decided which chicken he was going to kill for supper.

"Get that one," I told him, pointing to the fattest hen.

Quick as lightning, Meshomis seized the chicken and picked it up. He brought it to the wood stump he used for chopping firewood, pulled out his hunting knife and swiftly cut through the hen's neck, decapitating it in a flash. While the chicken jerked under his strong arms he said a short prayer of thanks to the animal for giving us its life.

Gran then sent me out to the garden to unearth some fresh veggies, the same garden where I got my celery and carrots for Little Red. Mom peeled the potatoes while Gran baked the bread. Uncle Wendall went out to milk Elsie, our cow, and churn some butter. My cousin David fetched some water, while my other cousin Wayne gathered firewood. My cousin Lola cooked the fresh veggies I brought back.

When everything was ready it was placed in bowls on the large table. Good manners were not a big part of dinner. You could keep your elbows on the table and reach across it to get whatever you wanted. You had to be fast in order to get your fill of food. Laughing and joking were common and all of us talked at the same time. This whole process took about three hours and we did it every night.

This night was different though, because Mom and I were going to drive to Manitoba the following morning and stay with my dad's parents. Mom took me to Winnipeg once a month to spend time with my grandparents but this was a special visit because Dad was coming home. I was going to meet my father for the first time.

"Bobbi," my mother said after dinner, "make sure you pack all your things. You know, we're going to see your other grandparents for a whole week!"

This was 1945 and my father had been overseas at World War II for four years, which was a long time for a three-year-old. Although I was looking forward to meeting him, for the most part I was a happy little girl without him. After all, how could I miss someone I had never met? I kept hearing about how I was going to meet him soon. Everyone raved about my father and about how wonderful he was.

"Yes, Mommy." I was dreading the long and boring car ride that would began early the next morning.

My paternal grandparents lived a six-hour car ride away, in another world, in the posh area of Winnipeg, Manitoba. As soon as we arrived at the Manitoba border, all the tall graceful fir trees from Ontario disappeared from sight and were substituted by fields of pale green shimmery wild sage and the odd tumbleweed. Meshomis had explained to me what a powerful medicine sage is, but it sure was boring to look at. At certain times of the year, there would be fields of bright yellow sunflowers coupled with purple flax, but not on this trip. There were no more big hills. Everything was flat, dry, sandy and hot, including the car. When I looked out the windshield, all I could see for miles was this straight flawless road that went on and on.

Mom realized how restless I was so she decided to tell me an anecdote. "Bobbi, when I was a little girl, I lived in Winnipeg for a while. It got so hot there that we used to drop eggs on the sidewalk." She paused to see if I was impressed yet. "And they would start to fry!

What do you think of that?"

Yeah right, I thought. Did she really think I was going to believe a story like that? But I was on my good behaviour so I didn't tell her my thoughts.

"Mom," I said, changing subjects, "it's a good thing we don't live in a city."

"Why is that, Bobbi?" she asked, giving up on the egg story.

"Meshomis says cities are cement jungles. And that people like money too much. They like money even more than they like the Creator!"

Apparently, this was the wrong thing to say. Mom got really tense and slapped me right in the face.

"Don't you dare talk like that in front of your father's parents. What a disrespectful little brat you are."

What did I say, I wondered, my cheek stinging. I never could figure out what I was supposed to say or do around Mom. I was always screwing up. It wasn't fair. Sometimes she would tell me to be honest and that my feelings were important, and then when I was honest about what I thought, she would slap me.

"Mom, you never want me to talk about Meshomis! I love my grandparents in Winnipeg and Meshomis, too!" That would show her, I figured.

Wrong. I got another slap right on the same cheek. Now it really hurt. Mom gave me the silent treatment for the rest of the trip.

When it came to the Priestsons, Mom had an inferiority complex the size of the moon. Whatever she deemed would be offensive to the flawless Priestson elite inevitably got me a swift slap to the face. The funny thing was that my father's family was the nicest group of rich people you could ever meet. But Mom was convinced that she was inferior to them.

After being cooped up in the hot suffocating car, looking out at boring sage for six hours, I had taken off my shoes to cool down. I had totally forgotten Mom's silly story about eggs frying on the sidewalk. When we arrived at the house I saw Grandma and Grandfather Priestson waiting to greet me, and I was so excited I barely waited for the car to come to a stop before I leaped out in my bare feet. The walkway was hot as a frying pan.

"Ow! Ow! Ow! Ow! Ow! Ow! Ow!" I cried, bouncing from foot to foot until I reached Grandfather, who picked me up. This was not a joyous arrival for me. I was not impressed with sun-fried sidewalks, the ground was way too hot here. And there were no woods to play in.

"Mommy, I don't like it here! Can we go back home where the Creator is not so mean?"

Mom's expression looked like she was going to slap me again, but she contained herself.

Grandfather's expression revealed that he was truly amused by my comment. He replied in a serious voice that showed me he understood my view completely. "Young lady, you certainly have a point about the hot cement. Sometimes, I simply can't understand God's logic. I remember burning myself on these sidewalks when I was a little tyke as well. You'll need to wear your shoes, my little princess, especially on nice hot days like today."

Grandfather's words made me feel better. He spoke to me like I was a grown-up, which made me feel important. I sat and talked with Grandfather in the den while Grandma laid the table for supper. Grandfather Priestson was as different from Meshomis as one could imagine. He was a distinguished old Scottish gentleman of eighty years, which made him old enough to be Meshomis's father. I told him all about Little Red and he certainly was impressed, especially that I had fed him from my own hands.

Soon Grandma called us in to eat. A formal dinner in the Priestson household was a high culture experience, to which Mom and I were total strangers. Mom had lived her whole life in the bush, until she met Dad. She didn't even know there was a thing called electricity until she was well into her teens. Grandfather Priestson came from a long line of important Scottish ancestry. Lining the walls of the dining room were huge, elaborate, serious portraits of Priestsons, who seemed to watch over us with a certain scold as Mom and I tried to eat with a little class. Behind my grandfather's imposing chair were portraits of Donald Priestson, Doctor of Medicine, coroner and founder of the Montreal General Hospital; and Neil Beith Priestson, my grandfather, who was an engineer with the Trans Canada Railway. There were women's portraits as well: Charlotte, Cathie, Amy and Marienette Priestson, all of whom were dressed in posh hats and fine long gowns and seemed as elegant as royalty.

The dining room had matching furniture: a maple hutch, a china cabinet and a table large enough to accommodate twelve guests comfortably. There was a delicate white linen tablecloth and we each had our own napkin engraved with the initial 'P' and a silver napkin holder into which our first name was engraved. The meal was placed on shiny silver platters with lids that bore the Priestson coat of arms. The cutlery boasted the same design. Everyone had three forks, two knives and two spoons, and my mother and I had no idea which went with what. The dishes, cups and saucers were all bone china and we drank out of crystal glasses. Everything was neatly placed on the table. Each person had his or her own tiny covered salt dish that held a tiny spoon with which you sprinkled the salt oh-so-fancilly. My grandfather cut the meat and my grandmother served the vegetables. If I wanted dessert, I had to literally eat all my vegetables. I dared not even dream of leaving the table without asking to be excused. There certainly were no chicken feathers lying around.

As my mother ate, struggling with her cutlery, she would sink into a depression. She was comparing herself to the classy Priestsons and thinking about her own heritage, which she considered utterly embarrassing and demeaning. She never seemed to be able to grasp formal etiquette. She had grown up in the woods, and she had no idea of finesse or trends or even of the existence of these things before she met the Priestsons. Every bit of finery she encountered in their house made her feel worse. She had been brainwashed by the nuns in the residential school that she and all Indians were savages. I now believe that she felt she was unworthy to even try to fit in with the Priestsons. Yet the Priestsons loved her dearly, never ever criticized her and always pretended they didn't notice her insecurities.

Grandma had prepared a delicious cold plate consisting of chicken, potato salad, green salad and fresh ripe strawberries for dessert. I ate to my heart's content and felt a tremendous amount of love for my grandfather. After dinner a wave of tiredness overcame me and Grandfather carried me upstairs and tucked me into bed.

"Grandfather," I yawned, "I like you."

"I like you too, my little princess. Goodnight."

The morning sun awakened me with its bright rays shining off the sparsely furnished bedroom I slept in when visiting Manitoba. Rubbing my eyes, I noticed I was still wearing my favourite little blue jumper and white silk blouse I had worn the day before. I had been so wiped out that nobody had the heart to disturb me by putting me into my pyjamas.

I was staying in my father's old bedroom, from when he was a child in the 1920s. I looked around at the antique furnishings in the morning sunlight that was creeping through the impeccably clean windows. All the furniture had been originally purchased by my great-grandparents in the 1800s. It was all authentic Victorian furniture. I lay on the bed and wondered about my ancestors, whose portraits hung on the dining room wall. I though of my great-uncles playing toy soldiers and wondered if they had to wear the fancy posh suits they were wearing in the paintings while they played. Grandfather had told me the night before that his sisters had all worn bustles when they were little girls, but I couldn't imagine trying to run and play wearing a long hoop skirt. I sure was glad I didn't have to.

There was a miniature antique maple table and matching bustle chair that my grandmother had told me I could use to have tea with my dolls. She told me that her father had made the set for her when she was a little girl so she could sit down comfortably to have a tea party with her dolls. The back of the chair was moveable to enable the bustle of her skirts to fit through. I didn't like playing dolls much but I did like sitting in the chair and looking at the table set because it was such a perfect size for me.

Dad had a monstrous four-poster bed. It held a huge feather mattress that I jumped on to get the day started. There was a gigantic seven-foot oak chest of drawers against the wall that seemed to swell with majestic pride. Its crown was artistically carved and crafted, giving it a regal look. I pulled out each drawer and gradually turned the chest into a flight of stairs. I climbed to the top to see what was up there.

Sitting up seven feet high atop the chest made me feel powerful—as though I were sitting on a throne, looking over my subjects with pride and utmost dignity. Above the bureau were some thick wood shelves, on which stood several polished awards Dad had won in the Boy Scouts. There were all kinds of shiny coloured pennants that he had won for tying perfect knots and for outstanding camping skills. He had a trophy for winning the high jump as well as another for track and field. The first trophy had a golden boy leaping sideways over a mesh net between two golden posts representing the high jump. The other one had a golden boy in a running stance and the engraving 'Presented to Robert Duncan Priestson for outstanding achievements.' I felt so proud. I couldn't read it myself, of course, but Grandfather had read it to me several times before on previous visits to Winnipeg.

Dad also had an army of toy soldiers on the chest which completely captivated me. They were carefully set up in various stages of action. I played with them much more than with my dolls. There was a small silver bell rattle on the corner of the bureau's surface and I rang it as a war call and made the soldiers come to the ready. From a small chest on the dresser, I took a stack of forgotten dominoes and built several forts so that my army could hide out from the enemy. I thought it was important that I do my best to protect all the soldiers from the bad guys.

I thought about how my dad was going to be coming back from the war soon. Dad had been overseas fighting for his country since I was still in Mom's tummy and I knew that any day now he would be coming back. Everyone always told me how perfect he was. Even Meshomis used to say to me, "Wait until you meet your father. He's an extraordinary man of talent and consideration. He's a superb human being." How was I going to compete with that? I didn't have any trophies. I thought about how Mom had told me that it would have been better if I'd been born a boy since my father would want someone to carry on the Priestson name, which I couldn't do. I hoped Dad would love me—even though I wasn't a boy, I was a tomboy and seldom played with dolls. What was going to happen to me when Dad came back? I worried I wouldn't be important any more and maybe nobody would have the time to love me because Dad would be taking everybody's time. Even though I was only three, I hated the feeling of losing my place in everyone's life. I could see myself being demoted to a nobody. A nothing. And everybody would dote on my dad, a total stranger. Worse still, maybe Mom would move up to second place, sending me to third. Or what if I got bumped behind my grandparents in rank and came in dead last, in fifth place, which has no ribbons or shiny golden trophies? I didn't like this idea at all. Furthermore, I didn't like the idea of Dad replacing Meshomis. As far as I was concerned, Meshomis was my father, grandfather and teacher and I wasn't going to change his rank on my list of favourite people. I worried about all these things while I played in Dad's old room.

I was also confused by the two sides of my family, especially the conflicting messages from my two grandfathers. My Indian grandfather, Meshomis, used to boast about my father. "Angekwe, always make your father proud of you," he had instructed. "You must never do anything to disgrace the Priestson name. Your father's a wise white man. He's accepted me as an Indian and he's helped me in many ways. We must always show gratitude for this." Conversely, my white grandparents used to tell me to be proud of my Indian heritage. On our previous visit to Winnipeg, Grandfather Priestson had sat me down for a serious discussion and stated, "Bobbi, your mother's family is just wonderful. It is important for you to learn everything you can about your Indian heritage so that you can honour your people when you grow up. Always be proud of being an Indian." All of this was nothing but confusion to me as a child. White. Indian. I did not understand the difference.

Once I finished jumping on the bed, playing with dominoes and soldiers, and worrying about becoming last place in the family, I ran downstairs to have a quick breakfast and then scoot outside to play. I wouldn't forget to put on shoes either, after that foot burning incident. It was a beautiful, cool and sunny day. On days like this, I'd wear my overalls, lie on the ground and let my imagination find all the different animals in the clouds. Then I would tote water from the puddles around the property with my little red pail to my sandbox and make mud pies à la Bobbi. But today, right after breakfast, as I was on my way out to play, Mom grabbed me by the arm and hauled me upstairs to dress me in a God-awful fancy white cotton dress embroidered with little pink flowers. I wanted to go outside and play but Mom made it perfectly clear that this was not going to happen.

"Listen here, kid!" she barked. "Today of all days, you are going to do exactly what I tell you and there will be no arguments at all." She added, "If you go outside, you can only sit on the porch swing. Understand?"

Roger! The porch swing was one of those big four-seaters that were about as much fun to a kid as being punished. She told me my other option was to stay inside and play with my dolls, which I didn't much care for either.

"Mom," I fussed, "why are you being so mean to me?"

"I am your boss!"

Mom's mood seemed to be in one of its unpredictable patterns so I shut my mouth. Altogether, it looked like that it was going to be a rough day. She sat me on my bed and started to put on my shoes.

"Today is the day you meet your father!" she snarled as she rammed on my patent leather shoe. "Remember I told you he had to go away, to fight for our country? Well he is finally coming home. Sit still, will you? He is anxious to meet his little girl and so you will stay—will you please sit still—clean. For the … damn … would you please … for the whole day and present yourself as a proper young lady."

I looked longingly out the spotless window of my room. A bird flew by. I wondered why Mom was so crabby on the day my father was arriving. You would have thought she'd have been in better spirits.

Staying clean was severe punishment. I went out to the porch, obeying Mom's order. I was standing on the boring swing. "Mommy, can I have a hug? I got butterflies 'cause I'm nervous about meeting Daddy."

"Behave yourself and stop whining," she said.

I decided I was going to be the best little girl that I could and sit on the swing with Mom. I sat on my hands so Mom wouldn't get mad at me for fidgeting. She was wearing a pale blue silk dress. Her skirt seemed to have yards of material in it. Her matching narrow blue belt made her waist look like an hourglass. Grandma had fixed her hair for her and loaned her some pearls. She even was wearing high heels and nylon stockings, which she never did unless she was going to church. She looked beautiful, I thought. As the swing swayed slowly back and forth, her hair gently brushed her face. She looked just like the Virgin Mary, except Mom's hair was dark. She was a nervous wreck though—picky about everything one minute and completely silent the next. My grandparents also seemed edgy. Grandma kept rearranging the table settings and Grandfather repeatedly went over to look out the window and he never worked on his crossword puzzle, which was his daily ritual. What a horrible day this was turning out to be. I was afraid to talk in case I said the wrong thing and got slapped.

Mom hadn't seen my dad since she was seven months pregnant with me and now I was three and a half. I asked permission to go upstairs to play with my dolls.

"Yes," she snapped.

I went upstairs and decided to do something special for Daddy. I was going to take Grandfather's advice and show I was a proud Indian. I went through my drawers and found my white wolf fringed shawl and the bone necklace that Meshomis had given me. I put them on and went to the mirror. Then I rummaged in Mom's makeup to paint my face. I had seen Meshomis put ashes and other things from the earth on his face when he participated in some sacred ceremonies so I knew it was important. I found Mom's lipstick which was perfect to draw two great big lines on my cheeks. I looked in the mirror again. I looked good! Then I put on my moccasins.

The phone rang as I started to walk back downstairs.

Grandfather answered and announced that Dad was on his way from the train station by taxi. Grandfather hung up the phone, looked at me and gave me the biggest smile I ever received in my entire life.

"Haiiyuh!" I affirmed loudly and stomped my foot on the ground. Mom, recognizing the chant all too well, looked over at me, scandalized. She gritted her teeth and came towards me like a hound. She jerked me by the arm and spun me round so fast the friction of my moccasins nearly started a fire on the hardwood floor. Well, I thought so, anyway. She hauled me to the washroom and washed my face so hard, the way you would a cat that's been sprayed by a skunk. I was afraid my hair would all be ripped out when she brushed it. Mom took off my white wolf fringed shawl, necklace and moccasins with a 'what in the world were you thinking' look and threw everything in the closet. The weather had become quite cool by now so she put on my yellow coat with the black trim, and then took me back outside to the swing and slammed my butt down on it.

"Don't move!" she commanded.

My grandparents and my mother moved to the front driveway and stood in a straight orderly line waiting one behind the other. I stayed on the swing following orders, but had a terrific view of the driveway. After a few minutes, a long black taxi drove up the narrow street and stopped in front of the driveway. A tall lean man in an army uniform got out of the passenger side. He then turned away and kind of skipped over to the trunk of the cab to get his luggage. He had his back to us as he reached to get his bags and paused before turning to face us, as though he were taking a deep breath.

I had a bad feeling that he was going to leap back into the taxi and take off. None of the other members of the family moved. Finally Dad walked towards us carrying his suitcases and I wondered if he would come and see me first. He was smiling and spoke in a low voice to Mom that I couldn't make out and then did the same with his parents but all the while he kept looking and walking towards me. I was still sitting on the swing. My heart was beating fast. The others remained so still, it was eerie.

Dad skipped up the three steps onto the porch and put down his luggage. I stepped off the swing and glanced over at Mom to make sure this was okay to do, but she wasn't even looking.

My dad bent down to me, gently mussed my hair and said, "Hello, young lady. I have been waiting to meet you for so long!"

He had the blackest hair in the world. He had beautiful clear blue eyes and such a wide genuine smile, just like Grandfather. I thought he was wonderful and fell in love with him immediately.

"Me too, Daddy," I said, and reached up and touched his hair.

Daddy turned to Mom and his parents and greeted them in what I later learned was a Scottish greeting, which was very reserved and stern. He shook his father's hand and pecked his mother on the cheek. They returned the same reserved greeting and blandly told him they were glad that he was home at last. It was difficult to believe they hadn't seen each other for over four years. However, Mom was visibly shaking. Dad grabbed her by the waist and spun her around. Still maintaining his dignified allure, he gave her a long kiss on the mouth.

"Leona," he said, "thank you for visiting my parents so often, and for giving me such a beautiful little girl."

Greetings being over, I figured I should be allowed to change into my overalls. I had been stuck in these fancy clothes quite long enough, I thought.

"Mommy, can I get changed now?" I whined.

Mom glanced over at Daddy to get his input on the matter.

"Young lady," he said, "how about getting some photos taken first so that we can all remember this wonderful day forever?"

What a drag, I thought, but I relented when Dad suggested I should get my favourite doll which could be in the pictures too. He sure was good at getting my cooperation. We took about ten million pictures and when that was finally over, I asked if I could change into my playclothes again. It was important, I thought, for my Dad to realize that I was a tomboy and that he and I could go fishing and do all kinds of boy things together. Anyhow, if me and my daddy were going to be buddies, I couldn't be expected to wear dainty little girl clothes. I remembered how Mom had told me that Dad wanted a boy to carry on his name, so I blurted out, "Daddy, Mom said girls can't carry on your name. I'm really sorry I'm a girl."

Nobody said a word or moved and I knew that I had blown it once again. I winced. Dad brought Mom over to me, and they leaned down to me. Dad cupped my little face and he had tears in his eyes.

"You and your mother are my two beloved girls," he said. "The moment I saw you, I knew you were exactly what I wanted. I love you very much, Bobbi." He then turned to Mom and said, "Leona, I don't care if we never have another child. As far as I am concerned, you have given me the greatest gift a man could ever receive and I dearly love our child." He added, "I have come to know her well through the loving letters you sent me."

By this time, everyone was crying except me. Even my stoic grandparents, who I thought didn't know how to cry, had some tears on their faces. I was overjoyed because my daddy loved me. I began dancing all over the room as I had seen Meshomis do when he got dressed up in full regalia at Indian powwows. Grandfather laughed loudly and said, "Your child is a breath of fresh air." I danced around in a circle, lifting one leg at a time, bent over, with my arms alternating. "Aye yuh yuh yuh! Aye yuh yuh yuh!"

Chapter Four

After Dad came back from the war, followed by a brief vacation, he continued his career in the army and I guess you could say we led a fairly normal military life. However, we got transferred to a new army base, Camp Petawawa, in Eastern Ontario. This meant a chaotic couple of weeks on the road and getting settled in the permanent married quarters which was housing for soldiers and their families. Poor Mom had never been away from Northern Ontario or Manitoba so when we found ourselves living in Eastern Ontario, approximately one thousand miles away from home, neither Mom nor I were impressed at first. I don't remember travelling to Camp Petawawa but I certainly remember the shock upon arrival. We were on a train, I think, although it could have been a bus.

"Mommy, where did the trees go? There aren't any trees. Mommy, are you listening to me? What am I going to do?"

I tugged on her blouse, whining about my fate, not even looking at her but instead staring at this vast mass of sand. Admittedly, there were a few trees but mostly what I would consider bushes. There were certainly no tall majestic cedar or birch trees. I was confused and wondered how I would cope with no one-legged friends to climb and play in. There was no verbal response from Mom. I glanced over at her, wondering why she wasn't answering. She sat there seemingly rooted to her seat. Tears were streaming down her beautiful face. Her brown eyes were filled with pain. I watched in amazement as she pulled herself together and replaced the pain in her eyes with hope.

"It's okay, Bobbi. This is a new adventure for all of us. We are going to meet a lot of new friends and life will be wonderful. We don't need trees to be happy. We have each other and that's what counts, isn't it?"

I don't think I ever felt as close to my mother as I did at that moment. And, do you know, it became okay. It certainly was different in Camp Petawawa but I met lots of kids and we had a ball, playing in the sand. Unfortunately, we only stayed there for about two years, until I was six, and then we got transferred again, this time to Montreal. Each new posting was a promotion for Dad.

That fall in 1948, at six years old, I started grade one in a Catholic Indian boarding school. My Dad sent me there believing that I was going to learn about the Indian way but that wasn't their way at all. I was taught that any kind of teachings I had received from a non-teacher or non-priest were completely irrelevant. I was told that the real God was in a church somewhere. I was confused by this, and I wasn't very receptive to the idea of spending so much time on my knees and learning all that catechism stuff. The nuns were hell-bent and determined to 'civilize' me.

"You will become a proper little lady of culture," they said. "You have been falsely taught by savages."

I didn't care what they said because I sure knew that Mom and Meshomis were not savages.

One day I snuck out of class to play outside, and I discovered a bed of clay. I found two worms in the clay, so I put them aside so they could watch me play. The worms reminded me of Ookashahgumme-kwe, and I didn't want to hurt them. I was dressed in a dark blue jumper with a white blouse, white socks and little navy shoes. My long dark hair fell to my waist in two braids. I had been permitted to keep long hair because the nuns knew Dad was white and he had stated quite firmly that his child would always have long hair. My clothing was covered with clay. When the nuns tracked me down, they were furious and ordered me to eat the two live worms as punishment. I looked at the nuns in disgust as I stood up. I put my little hands firmly on my waist and faced them with all the strength that I could muster. These sisters obviously weren't very smart. They wanted to punish me by killing Ookashahgumme-kwe, but I knew that neither one of those worms was Ookashahgumme-kwe because she was already dead. They were good little worms and were watching and learning from what I was doing. They were following the Red Path. The two sisters were certainly on the Black Path, for making me eat the worms. I tried my best to swallow them one at a time so they could just slide down my throat but I gagged them back up, still moving.

"Boy oh boy, I bet the Creator is really mad at you," I informed the two nuns.

Oops! That was definitely the wrong thing to say. They marched me back to the classroom. When we got there they placed me on my knees in the corner and I had to say the rosary ten times. However, I was on a roll, remembering Meshomis's teachings, so I took the trouble to inform the nuns that there was still time for them to change the path of destruction that they were on. "Hey, Sisters," I announced in my most self-righteous voice, "there is still hope for you. My grandfather told me that we can start to be good people when we know we've been bad, so maybe you could start now."

As a result of that outburst, I found myself seated on a high stool in the front of the room with a dunce cap perched on my head. The nuns told me that my chances of getting into heaven were the next thing to nil. That was okay with me. The last place I wanted to spend eternity was with a bunch of menacing-looking nuns.

While living in Montreal, something else happened that made me remember Meshomis's teachings, and made me decide to be kind to the less fortunate. It was because of this little kid, Heather, who lived in the same apartment block as I did, 1560 Boulevard Bourbonniere. We were both around seven at the time. She was built kind of square and had short curly dirty red hair. Her two front teeth were buck teeth, making her look like a horse. She was always dressed very raggedly. She looked like Little Orphan Annie. Her parents used to bring their fights with each other out into the street. None of the kids liked her but I felt sorry for her. Mind you, I didn't want the other kids to turn on me so I didn't bother with her much either, unless I was alone.

One day, my friend Georgie Pakowitz and I headed over to the corner store for a bag of chips. As we were walking along, I took this opportunity to ask him about her. "Georgie, how come nobody wants to be friends with Heather?"

He stopped walking and grabbed my hand. "Bobbi, don't be friends with her either, 'cause she's mean."

"Oh yeah, sure she is," I sarcastically replied. "Well, how come she's never been mean to me? Georgie, you are just being a nasty boy who hates girls."

"Bobbi, she came up to me for no reason and kicked me in the nuts, really hard. I even had to go to the doctor. All I said to her was that I liked her red shorts."

Well, I didn't believe that for a moment and was starting to feel really skeptical and defiant. I continued, "You probably did something nasty first. I think it's just awful how you and the rest of the gang don't want her around. I'm going to be nice to her, so there."

I should have remembered what Georgie said. A few days later, Heather invited me into her apartment to play because her parents were out drinking and she didn't want to be alone. We went into her bedroom to colour. Her room was almost empty and it was dark and gloomy. There was only one filthy little partly opened window. A piece of old cracked beige linoleum with faded roses partially covered the floor. The walls and the bureau were painted beige. Besides that, there was a little army cot with one skinny little pillow, that didn't even have a pillowcase, thrown on top of a threadbare sheet. Heather didn't have any toys but she had crayons and a couple of colouring books. We coloured for a few minutes until I accidentally broke a blue crayon. All I got to say was "Oh" before Heather had me in a choke hold. Pulling me over to the window with one arm, she grabbed my wrist with the other hand, threw my hand on the window ledge and somehow managed to slam the window down on my fingers. Ohhhhh, that was so painful. I slithered down to the floor in agony. I didn't even cry out. Tears rolled down my face.

"There," she said. "Now we are true friends."

Many emotions were running through me. I was thoroughly pissed off and hurting. I sure as hell did not have a feeling of friendship. I looked at her as if she was crazy. Trying to act tough, I yelled, "How in the hell do you figure that?"

"Well, Mom and Dad told me you have to discipline anybody

you care for so they will be good and do the right thing. That's why they have to punish me all the time. They tell me it hurts them more than it hurts me. I didn't used to believe them but now I do because I sure didn't want to hurt you. I almost cried when I knew I would have to give you the same punishment that I get when I break crayons."

"Well then, tell me why you kicked poor little Georgie in the nuts the other day. Your parents sure don't do that to you 'cause you don't got none."

Heather looked at me as if I was completely crazy, then said that her mother kicked her father in the nuts whenever he looked at her bust. She added that if Georgie had noticed her shorts he must've been looking at her bottom. She liked Georgie so she had to hurt him. I looked at her with my mouth hanging open. I didn't know what to say. She truly believed what she had said. Okay, now what? Maybe I should try to do everything I could to make Heather hate me, but I remembered Meshomis's teachings. Love is stronger than evil.

I reached over and hugged her and said, "You know what, Heather? I know you like me. Please don't hurt me anymore because if you do, I won't be able to be your friend anymore." I turned the conversation into a joke. "I screw up so much that if other people believed the way your parents do, I wouldn't be able to be friends with anyone."

I wasn't sure whether Heather understood what I meant but I got myself out of there and went home in a big hurry. I told my parents what had happened.

One evening shortly after, all the parents, with the exception of Heather's, made arrangements to get the kids together and go to St. Paul's Church basement for a meeting. My friend Georgie and I were terrified, wondering what trouble we had managed to get ourselves into. The rest of the kids skipped down the stairs into the basement, but Georgie and I held back, looking at the stairs as if they were the entrance to hell.

"Bobbi," Georgie whispered in my ear, "I think they must have found out I skipped school the other day. Yikes, am I ever in for it."

"You think you got troubles," I answered in an almost inaudible voice. "Well, I've got you beat. I went to Kresges the other day and stole an eraser. By the time I got home, I felt guilty and told my father and he marched me back to Kresges. He took me straight to the manager and I had to confess what I had done. Geez, did he ever give me shit." I felt sure the manager had somehow decided to throw me in jail.

"Get down here right now, you two," interrupted a firm, loud male voice. "We don't want to be here all night."

Oh my God, I just knew I was going to jail. Georgie was just as sure he was going to reform school. We crept down the stairs expecting to be raked over the coals. As we entered the room, we saw one long table had been set up, with the parents sitting on one side and the kids on the other. There were two empty chairs on the far end for us. My first thought was, 'Uh-oh, we won't have any chance to escape.'

Then I noticed that the adults all had cups of coffee and there were milk and cookies set up for all the kids. As soon as Georgie and I were seated, one by one the parents shared with us how important it was for us to continue to play with Heather and to be as kind to her as possible because she would be moving away soon and they felt it was important that she would always have memories of children who cared for her. They went on to explain that our kindness could help her learn a different way of life. We all objected strenuously because of our fear of her abuse towards all of us. The parents then explained that we had to arrange our lives not to be alone with her, and that we would be safe as long as we travelled in packs.

"Like wolves?" I asked, feeling all grown up.

"Yes, Bobbi," Mom answered, "just like wolves that are loyal and faithful and take care of each other."

I was impressed with my mom and loved her dearly at that moment because wolves are so important to Indian people. Meshomis had told me that following the teachings of the *mehegans* (wolves) would be an asset when I grew up.

The meeting adjourned a little later and we all went home. We kids felt safe after that, in packs like wolves. What we hadn't been told was that our parents had contacted the youth protection organization. They kept a close watch on Heather's welfare, and within a few months she was taken from her home due to physical abuse and neglect. I never saw Heather again, but at least she left knowing that a bunch of crazy kids in Montreal had cared about her. The next several years continued as before. Mom didn't handle living in Montreal very well and really began to abuse alcohol every chance she got. Her excessive drinking had started when we moved to Montreal. I guess it was just too much for a young woman from the bush to deal with the fast pace and indifference of city life.

I continued to attend school and tried to ignore Mom's drinking. I finished grades three, four and five at the same school, managed to make a few friends and graduated from Brownies. However, maybe because of Mom's drinking, I can't remember much from that time in Montreal between the ages of seven and eleven.

When I was eleven, one incident that happened in Montreal put me off bringing friends to my house. I remember bringing Bernice home after school. Bernice was this nice girl who was in my class. I always had lunch with her and she often invited me home to her place after school to play doll house. Eventually she started to complain that she never came to my house, so I obliged. Mom wasn't home at first, but she arrived drunk while we were in the living room exchanging tattoo stickers. Mom was teetering back and forth in the hallway, fumbling with her keys. Then she noticed us.

"Who in the hell is that?" Mom barked, pointing to my new friend Bernice.

Bernice sat straight up with a frightened look. I watched Mom in both amazement and shame, then said, "C'mon, Bernice, let's go in my room."

Mom stumbled over to the hallway table, stabilized herself, took a deep, deep breath and exhaled loudly, and looked at us again. Then this puzzled look came over her face. "Who the hell is that?" she barked again, with her index finger singling out Bernice.

She was so drunk she stumbled off to her room and shut the door. I was so embarrassed, and I had no idea how to apologize so I just dropped it altogether. What can you say to that when you're eleven years old? 'Please accept my apologies for my mom's behaviour,' I could've said. 'She's a lunatic!' There was no point in explaining. It was clear to Bernice and me that Mom was a lunatic.

Bernice suddenly remembered a chore she had to do and left for home. She never even spoke to me again.

I knew that Mom only acted like that when she drank. Her drinking always upset me and I wondered why the booze was so necessary to her when it made her act so terribly. I thought that maybe Mom believed the stereotypes about Indians all being drunks. I stopped bringing friends home after school and I fervently swore to myself that I would never abuse alcohol.

After many more embarrassing incidents involving Mom's drinking, Dad requested another posting to get us into new surroundings. He was hoping that relocating out of the cement jungle would help Mom with her drinking. So we moved from Montreal to Quebec City. This was the last of our yearly moves because my father had asked for a permanent position and it was granted to him. We moved, to my discontent, in the blistering cold of February 1954. This move was tougher than the others. My mother, although moody, had nevertheless always been a good woman in the strictest sense of the word. She's always been very giving and caring. But when she drank, I took on many burdens. Thus, things being as they were and although I was only twelve years old, I felt a lot older. I felt like Meshomis, except I wasn't nearly as cheerful and light on my feet as he was.

We moved into a medium-sized four-room apartment on Forget Street near St. Louis Road, a snowball's throw from a beautiful park called the Plains of Abraham, where Montcalm and Wolfe had their battle sometime in the 1700s. I used to go there whenever things got too hectic around the house. I liked the park because it had these great big maple trees and a bench where I could sit and watch the river flow.

Our apartment was quaint and warm and there was no one living in the flat next door, which meant we didn't have to hear the noise we had become accustomed to in Montreal. We had a charming dining and living room that stretched across the flat and was only separated by an arc that lined the ceiling, which gave the room a telescopic feel when viewed from one end to the other. My parents had the biggest room, which easily fit a king-size bed with space for their cabinets and mirrors and still plenty of walking-around room. My parents seemed pleased with it.

I had my own room. In it was my dainty pearl-white bedroom furniture, which included a brand new vanity table that stood in contrast with the pale pink walls. Many stuffed animals were propped up on my single bed as well as in every corner. I had a huge raccoon fur coat folded at the end of the bed that I used as a blanket. When I snuggled into the coat, I felt closer somehow to Meshomis.

Meshomis was still in Northern Ontario with his wife and other children. It seems to me that Meshomis never got older. He was always the same, full of wisdom and good advice and good spirits. I sat down on my raccoon fur and daydreamed of him. He was wearing his lumberjack jacket, worn-out blue trousers and steel-toe boots. I imagined him gently saying, 'Why do you always think that you need to be here to be happy, Angekwe? Don't you know the Creator has no preference as to where we live?' as he let out his warm laugh that always filled me with security and love. 'The Creator knows what He's doing, you know.'

I disagreed. Maybe the Creator had his head up his butt when He made me and when He created cities. He sure doesn't want to give me my way, ever, I thought. Maybe God don't make no junk except for me. The city was a place where too many people gathered to hurry and talk about all these things I knew nothing about. My mind briefly flashed to the Red Path but I pushed that out of my mind; the Red Path seemed so far away. I thought about how people here in Quebec City were so shallow. All they seemed to talk about here were musicians, and these Hollywood actors, and radios, and this and that. Nobody ever mentioned the maple trees and that nice little bench that overlooked the currents of the St. Lawrence River. It all seemed so superficial to me. The North was a place I could really connect to. The North was much better, indeed. I was stuck here for now and had to be alert to the evils of the city and not be too trusting. I sighed, but I decided to give Forget Street and our new apartment a chance. Out my bedroom window, through the flurries that were saturating the landscape, I could still see the park. And that's a pretty good thing, I tried to convince myself.

Unfortunately, I had to start school in the middle of grade six. The school building was about one hundred years old and made of stone. It was small and looked very posh, as if only really wealthy kids would be there. Talk about self-conscious. On my first day the teacher, Mrs. Cumberline, had me stand up in front of the whole class and "Tell everyone a bit about yourself." To make matters worse, when I said "I ain't got any brothers and sisters" she corrected me. "I don't have, Bobbi. I don't have any brothers and sisters." I knew that, but I was busy polishing my tough image so I wouldn't seem like a loser.

Some of the kids laughed. I took my seat beside Anthony Pollick, a twelve-year-old boy who answered every possible question the teacher could ask, not because he was eager to answer but because he was bored. Throughout the year, he would even correct the teacher sometimes. Anthony, I always thought, did homework before it was assigned. He was smaller than the other kids, and he was really smart and witty. On this first day, when some of the kids laughed at my grammar, he said to me, "Don't worry about them, Bobbi, they're still on the letter 'G' but hopefully they'll get to 'H' in a couple of days. Maybe even the letter 'I,' but since that's a vowel it could get tricky." He made me feel really special. I wasn't allowed to date guys yet, but I sure thought he was nice.

The night of my first day at school, my mother had me spend the evening joining the Girl Guide's association in order for me to meet potential friends.

"Bobbi, it'll be nice for you to meet other girls your age. You'll have fun, I'm sure of it," she said.

"But I don't even have a uniform! I'm going to look like an idiot!"

"No one will mind that you don't have a uniform. I can't imagine that anyone would pick on someone for something like that," she argued.

Dad drove me to the meeting, which was in the basement of St. Michael's Church, not too far from school. I wore a red dress and a white blouse. When I walked downstairs, I met the Girl Guide leader, Heather, who was dressed in a spiffy, fitted uniform. She introduced me to the other Guides with a lot of enthusiasm. Everyone looked great. They all wore the Girl Guide's blue blouse, dark blue skirt, blue beret and nice red scarf. Heather told me that it didn't matter that I didn't have a uniform; I had the prerequisites to becoming a Guide because I had graduated from Brownies back in Montreal, and I wasn't all that out of touch with the various Girl Guide procedures. The girls expected me to have a uniform the following week, which I did. Uniform or not, though, I would have to take the oath that night.

We all stood in a circle and raised our right hand and put our first three fingers up, holding our little finger with our thumb. Then everyone, except me, recited the Girl Guides Oath of Allegiance: "I promise … To do my best … To do my duty to God and the Queen …"

"No way am I pledging allegiance to her or any other member of her family," I stated loudly. "As far as I know, she disrespects Indian people, so I'll be damned before I make any pledge to her." Meshomis had told me how the Indian people had gone to war for Canada with a willing and patriotic heart. Upon their return, the Indians discovered that somebody—either the Queen's father or grandfather or the Indian agent, I couldn't remember exactly what Meshomis had said—had taken away their Indian status and they were now considered white men. That action was not well taken by any Indian. I felt proud of my grandfather's knowledge and wanted to share it.

I stood there with my little arms crossed, trying to look as much as possible like an Indian warrior even though I was inwardly terrified of being rejected.

The other kids appeared to be impressed with my defiance. My attitude didn't go over very well with Heather, but she let me get away with it. She told me she understood my feelings and said that I probably hadn't been taught about the importance of the Queen, seeing as how I was an Indian. Fortunately for her I restrained myself from kicking her in the shins.

Following the oath, we sat in a circle and Heather gave each of us a short rope and told us that today's 'interest topic' was going to be knot tying. Heather then proceeded to show us how to make various knots. Meshomis had taught me every knot there is and I could do all of them blindfolded if I wanted. I found it hard to believe that these kids didn't even know how to tie a boat to a dock. I felt so sorry for them that I jumped into Heather's presentation and showed them all the knots I knew.

"Bobbi," she said, "please be seated."

"But look! I can do all these knots," I pleaded. "Can I please help out?"

Heather examined my knots and saw that I knew what I was doing so she let me help. I felt proud. Inwardly, I gloated.

After the meeting, we all sat around chatting in the back hall. The girls were nice but they seemed overly preoccupied with singers and about how they just had to see Marlon Brando in some stupid movie. They were also blabbing about Audrey Hepburn starring in another idiotic show. One of the girls said I looked just like her, and a series of yesses followed.

There was one girl who really caught my attention. Her name was Audrey. She was sitting at the table with the other girls, and her uniform had several emblems sown on it. It was the same uniform as everyone else's, except Audrey had undone her scarf slightly, which gave her a splendid look of aloofness, which I liked. She barely said two words all night.

At eight-thirty we were dismissed. Dad was already waiting for me upstairs. I was happy to get home. By then it was nine o'clock and since I had nothing to do and no one really to talk to, I went to bed.

I was pretty lonely at that time. In part it was because we kept moving from place to place, which caused me to have to make new friends everywhere we went. More importantly, the reason why I wasn't making any friends was directly due to my mother's drinking. I'm sure I would have been good at making friends. But I knew that at some point I'd have to invite them over and then they'd meet Mom, which would be a certain disaster if she was on a drunk. I could never predict when Mom would drink. All I knew is that her 'episodes' were becoming closer together and lasting for longer periods of time.

Having few close friends, I felt isolated most of the time. Whenever I mentioned my loneliness to my parents, they wrote it off as a puberty thing. They blamed all of my feelings on puberty. At the time, I had absolutely no idea what puberty meant; I figured I had some kind of a horrible disease that was probably fatal. I was confirmed in this belief when I got my monthly visitor for the first time. The cold feeling I had when I saw the blood was both terrifying and a relief. I panicked a little. To make sure I didn't get any blood in my bed and underwear, I stuffed about a whole roll of toilet paper in my panties. I didn't want to tell Mom in case she would get mad at me. And I just couldn't tell my father—that would have been far too embarrassing.

Instead, I wrote about it in my journal.

> 11 February 1954
> Dear Diary,
> I'm dying. What a crappy life this turned out to be. I always knew I was different in some way. My half Scottish, half Indian blood is finally failing me as I always suspected. I've put some toilet paper on the wound to slow down the blood, but it doesn't seem to change anything. I'm sitting down harder than usual to put pressure, too.
> Bobbi

> 12 February 1954
> Dear Diary,
> Still slowly bleeding to death. Still using lots of T.P. I haven't told Mom or Dad yet. I don't want to worry them. They'd probably blame themselves for mixing blood—a deadly combination. Tomorrow I will tell my new friend, Angela, about my impending death. Mom has asked about the toilet paper. She said it's the third roll she's replaced in two days.
> Bobbi

> 13 February 1954
> Dear Diary,
> Apparently this bleeding business is normal. Angela told me all about it. It's called menstruation-something-or-other and it's the pits. Angela said I needed to ask my mom for a "pad." A pad of what, I'm sure I don't know. I'm not dying.
> Bobbi

I asked Mom for a 'pad' and she knew immediately what I was talking about. When I told her about the toilet paper, she laughed in a Meshomis-like way. She then told me all about 'the visitor.'

"What do boys get?" I asked.

"Well, Bobbi," Mom was uncomfortable, but went on, "boys get ... well ... white stuff."

"White stuff?!"

Well good, I thought. At least something horrible happens to them, too. For a moment I had a lightning flashback to something in my past but I didn't grasp what it was. Funnily, Mom never told me that the visitor was a monthly thing and when it happened again, a month later, I panicked. I asked Mom if she had any idea why I was getting the visitor a second time. She went into gales of laughter and didn't explain further.

Chapter Five

A couple of weeks following my first Girl Guide's meeting, I was alone in the kitchen getting my homework ready. It was 7 p.m. and I was wondering whether this was really going to be the last transfer for Dad. I wondered whether Mom would ever stop drinking. I felt so lonely and alone in a big cruel world.

'This just isn't fair!' I told myself over and over. I plunked myself down at the kitchen table to begin my lessons. Both my parents were out. Dad was out with his army buddies celebrating his promotion to sergeant in the Royal Canadian Ordinance Corps. I had no clue where Mom was at the moment and I was too miserable to care. As soon as I finished my school assignments I wandered off to bed. I had just nodded off to sleep when I heard Mom stumble in.

That night Mom arrived home first. As she staggered around trying to find her bed, I awakened for just long enough to decide that she must have been drinking again then drifted back to sleep. I didn't hear Dad come home from the bar some time later. Neither Mom nor I knew that he brought an old homeless man with him. Without asking for my mother's permission, he gave him the couch to sleep on. When Mom woke up the next morning, she didn't expect to find a stranger in her living room. She shrieked bloody murder. I sprang out of bed faster than I ever had before and ran straight to the kitchen from where I'd heard her scream. To my amazement Dad was already there. He thought she had damn near killed herself or something.

"Who in the world is that?" she yelled at Dad, in a panic. "What in the world is going on here, Bob?"

"Oh," Dad said, visibly relieved that Mom was not hurt. "That's Gramps."

Mom's face contorted into a twist and her makeup from last night, which she had neglected to wash off, looked like it had been applied with a sling shot. She had crusts of mascara caked under her eyes and smudged lipstick. Her hair was all wrapped into rollers and she had on this old raggedy blue terrycloth bathrobe and big floppy slippers. Dad was standing there in a tank top and boxer shorts with his hair standing out every which way. I took a quick glance at myself, too. None of us looked very flattering.

"Bob," Mom muttered, "do you realize that I could have walked into this room in a negligee, or even worse stark naked?"

"Ha ha ha ha ha ha ha!" I laughed at the thought of such a scene.

"Leona," Dad answered, "listen, I know that this isn't a normal situation, but I also know that you would've never forgiven me if I hadn't brought this elderly gentleman home. Look, sweetheart, this man is down on his luck, but you'll see that he is very well educated and quite articulate. He's just down on his luck and has nowhere to go."

I wondered if Mom was going to buy into this line of horse manure.

"He's homeless?" she asked.

"Yes."

"Oh my goodness, the poor creature. I'll make him breakfast right away."

I realized I must have flown past this old guy in my hurry to rescue Mom, so I cautiously wandered back to the living room to have a look at him. There he was on the sofa, just as my mom said. He looked like Santa Claus on welfare. He had a big dirty white beard and rosy cheeks and a bright bulbous red nose. There appeared to be a big fat belly under the blankets. Amazingly, he was still sound asleep, despite Mom's scream.

"I guess when your beard turns white you go deaf at the same time," I muttered under my breath.

As I stood staring at him, he opened his eyes. He kind of hauled himself sideways to sit upright, which took everything out of him. It was a terrific struggle but finally his body rolled itself upright. Then he started making these grunting sounds which turned into throaty, phlegmy coughs. It was quite disgusting. He looked up at me and smiled, but his teeth were in a glass of murky water on the side table beside him.

"Well, hello there!" he said, slipping his teeth into his mouth. "Who might just you be?" he asked.

"Bobbi," I said.

"Well, Bobbi," he said thoughtfully, "I am definitely going to enjoy getting to know you."

The leer he gave me was terrifying. I felt a shiver run up my spine. I didn't know why, but for a moment I felt my mind briefly flash back to another time. I felt a memory but didn't see one. I stood frozen in fear, unable to think or move.

Dad's gentle touch on my shoulder took me out of this frozen state and he asked in a low voice, "Honey, is anything wrong?"

"Huh?"

"You've been standing here staring at our guest," he said, smiling gently.

"Huh? I'm fine, Dad. Sorry."

I walked away quickly and got dressed for school. I knew one thing, this old guy was weird. We all sat down to breakfast. My parents informed me that I should refer to our new guest as 'Gramps.' Mom served breakfast. Gramps ate a lot.

"Are you done with that paper, Bob?"

"Sure thing, Gramps. Here you go."

"Oh I just love to read the paper. Really gets my day started on the right foot."

'Gramps' opened the paper and began reading. Dad leaned in to me and whispered, "Bobbi, now is a perfect time for you to put our teachings to work. We have a guest in our home now, so you must always treat your elders with respect and obedience."

"Yes, Dad, I know. Thank you for reminding me." Respect and obedience surely was the pitfall of childhood. It was so irritating to always be reminded how to behave.

My home was close enough to the school to walk, which took me about fifteen minutes depending on my mood. I had become accustomed to walking to school with my new friend Audrey. I had noticed her walking to school and remembered that we had met briefly at the Girl Guide meeting the week before; she was the quiet girl who loosened her scarf. As it turned out, she and I were neighbours. We lived three blocks apart, went to the same school and were in the same grade, though in different classes. She was in Mr. MacMillan's class and I was in Mrs. Cumberline's, the one who was continually on my case.

At first, Audrey had avoided me. The first time I saw her walking, she stayed on the other side of the street and though I kept looking over at her, furtively trying to make contact, she kept looking forward all the way to school. The second day she did exactly the same. On the third day she wasn't there. On Friday I was walking along, but I kept looking back to see if she was coming or not. Eventually I saw her in the distance, fifty yards or so behind me. I recognized her long dark-blue hooded coat and red boots. I decided to stop and wait for her. When she got close enough I lifted my right arm amicably and said, "Hi there! I'm Bobbi. Weren't you at the Girl Guide meeting last week? I'm new here."

She stopped and tilted her head to the side and said, "Yeah. You're the new girl, right?"

"Yeah," I said, smiling. We stood for just a moment with nothing more to say, but I was really excited that I was making a new friend.

"Wanna walk together?" she asked.

"Sure!"

Audrey had this monotonous tone of voice, as though nothing ever phased her. She also had this beautiful thick dark-brown hair and rosy cheeks from the cold winter air. We took it upon ourselves to meet at the corner of Forget Street every morning to walk together, and every afternoon we met in front of the school principal's door to walk back. We talked about everything, except about our parents at first. And I told her all about the North and the moving around, and about Meshomis.

Audrey was born in Quebec City. Her dad was English speaking but her mom was bilingual, so Audrey spoke French pretty well by virtue of being around it. Our neighbourhood was a bilingual one and she had made some friends in the neighbourhood who spoke only French. Audrey kept to herself in many ways. She didn't talk or move much. Dad liked Audrey a lot and said she had the air of a calm river. She wasn't excited or jumpy like me, but she did like the park in front of my house and she'd go there sometimes by herself to think about things. She was always composed, but had the ability to be very sarcastic and funny.

That morning when my parents had been lecturing me about respect and obedience, I asked her, "Audrey, do your parents think you're an idiot? I am so sick of mine always being on my case. This morning they gave me their Don't-Forget-Your-Teachings-about-Honour-and-Respect speech because we have this old geezer called Gramps staying with us. Jeez."

"Who's staying with you? Like, your grandfather?"

"No, no. Both my grandfathers are magnificent," I said proudly. "This here old guy is called Gramps but he's no relation. My dad brought him home from the bar last night."

"Well, at least you have a father. Mine died when I was a kid." She paused and then added, as monotonously as always, "And my mother drinks all the time."

"Mine too!" I replied with a cheer of team spirit, then quickly composed myself and sympathized about her dad.

It seemed that I wasn't the only kid in the world with an alcoholic parent, and I decided right then and there that it would be okay to bring Audrey home after school. She loved coming to my house after school because her mom was usually depressed and when she was drinking she was abusive. Her father had died of a heart attack when she was four years old. She missed him a lot, she said, but by now she was used to him being away. She said her mom cried almost every night and that she tried to be there for her but her mom kept rejecting her. Apparently, once she even blamed Audrey for her dad's death by saying that if he hadn't had to work so hard to support the family, he would still be alive.

When Audrey came home with me the first time, Mom wasn't in and Dad was at work. But Gramps was there all right. He seemed really surprised to see us and commented, "Well! An extemporaneous visit! It is always a pleasure to meet new people. Call me Gramps."

"This here is Audrey, Gramps. She's my friend from school."

"Pleased to meet you, Audrey."

Mom came home while Gramps, Audrey and I were sitting around the kitchen table. Gramps insisted on telling us a "transmogrifying episode" about his life. Mom sat down with us. She was sober.

"I wasn't always an itinerant," Gramps began his story. "I used to be rich, to tell you the truth. Alas! My story goes back quite a ways, quite a ways. I was born Walter R. Ross, in the Orkney Islands, Scotland. My mother and father left the old country in 1882, when I was only three years old. Hard to believe a man of my grandeur could've ever been three years old, isn't it?" He looked at me and Audrey for confirmation. Not getting it, he continued. "Well, I was a heck of a kid, apparently, according to my parents, always getting into scrapes and the like.

"We boarded a boat to Canada. Many went to the U.S., but my father preferred it right here in Canada. He said it had better prospects. He was right to some degree, but wrong in others. We moved to Halifax, Nova Scotia—that's where the boat dropped us off, and Dad decided to get work right there and then. We lived there for about four years, I guess.

"My mother died of typhus when I was eight years old. That devastated me and Dad. You never met anyone so thoughtful in your life as my mother. She'd always help me in my lessons. Made sure I always got good grades. Made me study. Made me read inordinately, a habit I never broke, really. Dad … well … he was a fisherman. Left the house for days at a time, came back with money and lots of fish, naturally. You never saw so much fish! We dreamed of fish, we ate it so much. Mom could cook the heck out of anything and she must've had a hundred recipes for fish and it seemed we never ate the same meal twice, even though Dad was bringing the same old fish home every week. Anyway, Mom died, God bless her soul, and … well … Dad wasn't able to cope with it very well. She died on March 23, 1887. I guess as homage to her, exactly four years later, on March 23, 1891, I got home from school and found my father hanging in our basement. I was a big kid and so I was able to get my father down from the beam he'd hung himself off and tried to revive him, but he was gone. God bless him.

"The authorities, they got me and inquired whether I had any other family I could live with, or else I'd have to go through an adoption system. I told them I had an uncle in Montreal and so I went there to live with Uncle Jeffrey until I was sixteen years old. My uncle was into the shipbuilding business and he took me under his wing and I learned everything you could ever possibly know about the shipbuilding business.

"Eventually, at twenty years old, I got married to Ellen and I got a nice house in Montreal. Unfortunately, she passed away shortly after our marriage. I remarried a few years later in 1910 with a beautiful young woman, ten years my junior, named Gwendolyn. Ah, the beauty and sweetness of that woman was uncanny, until I lost my fortune and was reduced to rags."

Here Gramps threw up his arms in an exclamatory, innocent way.

"I never saw it coming," he continued. "She was the sweetest thing and then one fine day—poof!—she was gone. Gwendolyn ran off with some American business mogul. Never saw nor heard from her again.

"Anyway, the blow was too much for me, so I started travelling around, getting into adventures here and about, and I never stopped. I decided I was going to see the world altogether. Been drifting for a long time now. Sure, I got work all over the world. I could tell you a thousand stories. And well, I've been here in Quebec City for a while now and I'd have been on my way, I think, if you generous people hadn't so graciously taken me in. I don't know how I'll ever repay you. I mean it. I am very grateful."

"Think nothing of it, Gramps," my mother interjected. "You're most welcome here, you know? Most welcome," she added as she wiped the tears from her eyes and cleared the table. Everyone, including Audrey, thought Gramps was an interesting and fascinating old geezer and since he was nice to me I decided I had no reason to be frightened of him.

One thing about Gramps' story is that I heard him tell bits and parts of it over and over again and I noticed that they changed in some ways. At any rate, the dates changed. I think Dad noticed too; one time he looked over at Mom and me to see whether we had also noticed. I guess Dad simply thought that Gramps was old and may have lost a few marbles along the way.

One Friday evening my parents invited Gramps to accompany them to a house party taking place down the street. The neighbours were having a goodbye party because they were moving to Belleville, Ontario.

"So, Gramps," said my father congenially, "what do you say? Would you do us the pleasure of accompanying us to the Pollicks'?"

Gramps looked pensive and took on a calm, almost sad voice as he said, "As you know, I love children and never had any of my own. I think your little girl is just an amazing human being and if it is okay with you, I would find great pleasure in being her guardian during your absence. I would love to take the time to get to know her better. It has been so long since I have felt part of a family."

They agreed to let him babysit me. I felt uneasy. Something was wrong with this picture. I stood at the kitchen window and watched my parents leave. When I turned around, Gramps was staring at me.

"Well Bobbi," he said, "your parents won't be back for a while so go on and get washed up and ready for bed and then you can come back and see me for your cleanliness inspection."

This was likely the most bizarre request I had ever heard. I thought it had to be a joke or that maybe I had misunderstood him.

"Oh, I'm already ready, Gramps. I think I'll just do some homework in my room for a while, if that's okay."

Gramps' face got stern and menacing and he grabbed me by the arm and squeezed it, "Listen, you bitch, I'm not going to get a headache from you tonight, so do as I say!"

As soon as I heard the word 'bitch' I realized that my initial apprehension towards Gramps had been right on. I went to the bathroom to get cleaned. I felt sick and cold all over. While I was in the bath he banged on the door, startling me and causing me to have shortness of breath. Shaking, I sat in the bath and looked at my body, noticing how skinny it was, how small I was, and how I wouldn't be able to out-fight Gramps. I realized that I was not a woman, but a girl. I had no breasts, no curves. I was barely pubescent. My knees were purple from fright.

"Hurry up!" he ordered, banging on the door.

I felt paralyzed by fear. Putting my bathrobe over my naked body, I went to the raggedy blue couch where he was waiting for me. I had no idea what to expect, but I had rarely felt so alone in my life.

"Take off that robe!" he yelled.

He was breathing loudly, wheezing, and he had an insane look in his eyes. They reminded me of Uncle Stinky's, which filled me with a deep sense of dread even though I couldn't remember exactly why.

I took off the robe.

"Sit down!"

I sat down on the couch, pressing my knees together and leaning over my legs with my upper body to save my dignity. Gramps' sleeping quarters were absolutely disgusting. Even the water where he kept his teeth was grosser up close. It looked as though all the germs from the teeth were trying to crawl up and out of the glass but died on the way and were rotting on the sides. His pillowcase was stained in many different shades of filth. His bag of belongings reeked and was absolutely gross.

"What do you think of this, Bobbi?"

He was holding out his penis, shaking it. His fat, hairy belly was bulging out from his unbuttoned shirt; his pants and underwear were down to his ankles, revealing a great mass of grey pubic hair that seemed to cover the whole of his body.

All I could think about was that it looked like a old shrivelled-up turkey neck. Mom always refused to even touch the turkey neck when cooking the bird at Christmas.

"I really don't know, Gramps," I said.

"You're going to lick it and suck it or I'm going to backhand you like you've never been backhanded before! Got that?"

I wanted to cry, but I couldn't. He shoved himself in my mouth and I gagged and vomited on him. He didn't hit me, but he got angry and pinched me in the crotch very hard. I yelled out in pain. He walked away, cleaned up the vomit and came back with a banana in his hands.

"You will learn to suck my cock."

He gave me the banana to practise on and coached me until I could do it fairly well, I guess, then he made me continue on his penis. He kept calling me a stupid bitch throughout. Suddenly he grabbed his penis from out of my mouth and started jumping all over the room yelling, "Hallelujah, Hallelujah, what a great blow job." Released, I ran to the bathroom. I felt so dirty. I scrubbed the inside of my mouth raw with my toothbrush and baking soda.

I was way too scared of him to tell my parents because he told me that if I said anything to anyone, he'd get me real good, so I'd better watch it. By the look in his eyes, I knew he would really hurt me if I said anything. My parents went out six times that month and the abuse occurred every time. Amazingly, I was able to tune out the horrific events and to continue on, life as usual. I didn't tell anyone about it, but I somehow knew that I would figure out a way to get rid of this disgusting excuse for a human being. I had to get rid of Gramps. And I vowed vengeance on him.

Gramps was a great actor. He'd call me 'bitch' or 'whore' when my parents weren't around and call me an 'august doe' in front of them. Audrey noticed how distant and silent I had become during this time and asked me what was wrong, but I just told her that I thought I was sick or something. I don't know if she believed me. Those of us who have been abused can tell when someone else has been too, so I don't know if she knew or not. I stopped bringing her home after school. Instead, I would go to the park across from our apartment and sit on the bench until suppertime, thinking of ways to get back at Gramps, about how I was going to get rid of him. I thought for a month and described the situation in my journal:

> 2 March 1954
> Dear Diary,
> I cannot tell anyone about what is happening. Gramps is a monster. All he ever calls me is 'bitch' and he makes me do things to him. I hate him. I will spend as much time at the park as I can to avoid him.
> Bobbi

> 6 March 1954
> Dear Diary,
> I am a prisoner in my own house. Gramps continues to call me 'bitch.' This is his name for me! Respect and obedience for my elder means nothing to me anymore. I wish Dad would

kill Gramps and throw him in the river. Maybe I could kill him. I would love to. I hate him. Audrey is wondering about me, but I cannot tell her, either. Last night Mom and Dad went out again. Gramps made me do it to him and told me to swallow. I didn't. I won't. I will bite it off!!!!
Bobbi

18 March 1954
Dear Diary,
Dad is out again, but I hope he will be home soon. Gramps did it again. He tried to put it in me this time, but didn't. It hurt. I'm going to kill him. I have taken a kitchen knife and placed it under my bed. Tonight I will use it on him while he sleeps. I will take it and stab it through his big, fat, hairy belly and twist it until he squeals like a pig.
Bobbi

Suddenly, I had the solution as to how to stop it all. I was sitting on the park bench watching the river flow when I remembered Dad saved his pennies in a drawer of his desk in his room. I decided that the next time my parents went out, I would tell Gramps that Dad had asked me to tell him to take the pennies for himself because Dad had decided he should save quarters, not pennies. I ran home. It was three-thirty, plenty of time to execute my plan. Mom wasn't home and Dad was still at work. I walked straight into my parents' room and opened the drawer where Dad saved his pennies. My heart was beating fast. I took out the penny jar and brought it to the kitchen.

"Gramps?"

"What is it?"

"My father asked me to tell you that you can have his pennies to get back on your feet." I showed him the jar of pennies. Gramps looked at me with interest.

"He says that he isn't going to save pennies anymore, he's going to save quarters instead. So he thought you might want them." I poured the pennies onto the table. Gramps fell for my lie. He looked at me and went "Humph," then scooped up the pennies and walked back to his couch. He forgot about me while he counted the twenty dollars that he thought was now his. I watched him put the coins into a pair of navy blue socks and carefully place the socks under the couch. Now all I had to do was get my father to notice Gramps' thievery. I knew he wouldn't stand for it. I waited outside to meet Dad when he returned home from work. He got out of his car and saw right away that there was something on my mind.

"Honey, what is it?"

I feigned deep concern as I lied, explaining with an innocent face that I had seen Gramps steal his pennies.

"Where is the money now, Bobbi?" Dad asked, holding me lovingly by the shoulders.

"In a pair of navy blue socks. Under the couch!"

Dad believed me without question. He immediately entered the house, went straight to the couch, leaned over and fished out the socks. Gramps stood by, wondering what was happening.

"Gramps, you've stolen money from me. How dare you treat me with utter disrespect after everything we've done for you."

The look on Gramps' face was more exhilarating to me than Christmas morning. I knew that he knew that he had been outsmarted by a twelve-year-old girl. He looked at me in a fury, but quickly checked his demeanour, not to get caught by my dad.

"Bob ... Bob, I can explain everything."

"I have no doubt of that," Dad said, "but it won't be necessary. Take your things and leave this house immediately."

"But Bob ... please be reasonable and let me explain."

"Immediately!" Dad lifted his right hand, indicating that there would be no discussion about it.

Gramps accepted his defeat and I watched him grudgingly pack his bag and walk out the front door without the twenty dollars' worth of pennies. It was the single greatest victory to watch him leave never to be seen again. I was free at last.

The next morning I met Audrey on the way to school.

"Hey. What are you so happy about?" she asked. I had never told her about Gramps except that I didn't like him.

"Gramps is gone for good. He just left last night!"

"So you're not sick anymore, huh?"

"No, I feel great!"

Until my experience with Gramps, my intention in life was to be kind to others because I was taught that unless you have walked a mile in someone else's moccasins, you can't know where they are coming from. But the Gramps situation had called for drastic measures and I am proud of that victory. It left me changed inside. Yes, it certainly did.

How I had set up that old pedophile was my first real taste at manipulating others to get my way. It was to lead me later to become sneaky and underhanded, with an attitude of 'I gotta get you before you get me.' Despite my original intentions I truly became Ookashahgumme-kwe's staunch and faithful follower; I too became powerful and capable of hurting. The strange ideas of love, forgiveness and acceptance eventually became distant obscure concepts to me.

For years, raging with pent-up anger and hate, I made very precise decisions as to where I was going, what I was going to do when I got there, when I was going to do those things and with whom, and where and why I chose the particular people, places and things. At times it was uncanny how I could twist things around so that circumstances looked like they were anybody else's responsibility other than mine.

I learned how to play the victim role to perfection and oh how I played it, along with any other role that would be beneficial to me. Me, me, me—that's all that was important, no matter how I achieved it. I called all this: 'putting on the appropriate masks.' It worked beautifully for a while, too, and it was a great way to camouflage my inner and true feelings. But at the same time it was hell on the psyche.

After experiencing the horror I went through with Gramps, the path of my life became twisted, with many forks and detours. It was not the way I had visualized it. My plan had been to travel life on a beautifully paved four-lane highway. Now it looked like I was going out of control, full speed ahead, on a small dirt road with no directions and many detours. The detours, when things didn't go my way, or when I had to take the consequences for my actions, turned out to be a frustrating constant.

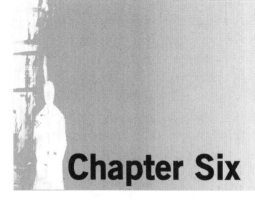

Chapter Six

While living on Forget Street in Quebec City, Mom's drinking got worse and worse. By the time I was twelve, it was no big surprise for Mom to be away from home for days at a time. She would go out with the intention of meeting some friends for a couple of drinks and she would end up going on a binge, not coming home for three or four days. When she'd come back, she would re-assume her role as a wife and as a mother. She never would explain where she had been. Later, I would discover she was a blackout drinker—a person who loses their memory after a few drinks. However, often when she came back from a binge, she would stop drinking for weeks at a time. She would quit long enough for things to get back to normal again—and then go back out.

During this time, Dad seriously contemplated leaving Mom. One evening he came into my room and sat down on the edge of my bed to tell me that he and Mom were going to have to live apart from each other. Dad wanted the both of us to start a new life apart from Mom because her drinking was too hard to bear. Despite her never drinking in front of him, he was aware of how it was affecting me. The parents of a friend of mine from school had separated, so I had heard about this type of arrangement. I lay in bed and listened to my father without saying much. Later that night I woke up sobbing and when Dad came into my room to see what was wrong, I begged him over and over again not to leave. He decided to stay, and today I know that it was for my sake.

During her binges, my mother would go out and buy new television sets on credit and then sell them on the black market. She did this to have more money to drink. Not only televisions, either. She made very good use of her credit cards. After a while, we didn't have any money to afford nice things, including the rent. Desperate and not knowing what else to do, Dad moved us to another neighbourhood in Quebec City. We moved from Forget Street in Sillery to Limoilou, where things looked older and a little more unkempt and the rent was much cheaper. Limoilou was clearly a step down from Sillery. It had none of the charm or greenery that Sillery offered. But moving to a different area had the benefit of separating my mother from her drinking buddies, increasing the off-chance possibility of her quitting altogether. The longest she stayed sober, before she stopped drinking for good a few years later, was after moving to Limoilou. She went six months. We moved to Limoilou in February 1955, right next door to St. Peter's Anglican Church. I had just turned thirteen and I was in grade seven at Quebec High School. I began making new friends at high school, most of them older than me.

My logic told me that I was the cause of my mother's drinking for the following reasons: first, she had told me a hundred times that I was a mistake, should never have been born and that I should have been a boy and so on; second, I was around the house more than Dad so I thought that my proximity had some terrible effect on her. Seeing that I was the catalyst of it all, I decided I should try to help the situation.

Thinking that maybe God could help, I went to seek help at the Baptist church. I spoke to a minister there and told him everything. I told him how Mom left for days at a time, sometimes coming in stumbling and knocking things over and screaming and crying and spending all Dad's money on booze and that was the reason we were in Limoilou, and so on. That nice minister sent one of his colleagues to visit Mom. He came over to the apartment and lectured Mom on how sobriety would be beneficial to her and her family. This occurred during the day, while I was at school. When I arrived home after school, Mom greeted me at the door and she had the same look on her face as she did when I got all dressed up in Indian attire the day my father came home from the war. Except that this was much worse. I didn't even have time to enter the apartment. She was in the doorway screaming, "Who in bloody hell do you think you are, going off and telling stories about me to the local minister? Shame on you! Don't you have any idea about anything? You don't go and tell strangers about our business! It's our business! You need to start being more intelligent, Bobbi. Shame!"

She followed me to my room and continued to scream "Shame!" while pointing her index finger at me and rubbing it with her other index finger. Regardless, later that month, on September 13, Mom stopped drinking, probably out of pure embarrassment. She stayed sober for a few months but in February, on my fourteenth birthday, she started again. It took no time for her to start binging and coming home stumbling all over again. It was like she had never stopped at all.

When I was fourteen, I stopped caring about whether or not Mom was drinking. I decided to live it up. This is when I really started to change. I started to go out more and as most of my friends were older than me, we would end up going to bars. While the others drank Manhattans and Pink Ladies, I drank Bacardi and Coke, which was my first and favourite drink. Mind you, I would only have a couple a night, lest I turn into my mother. My most noteworthy friend at the time was Marylin, seventeen, who was by far the prettiest and the leader of the group. She had a fantastic body and a gorgeous face. She had enormous, soft blue eyes and shiny blond hair that she wore it up in two cute clumps on the sides of her head. Edith, also seventeen, was the tough girl of the group and highly sarcastic. She sometimes reminded me of Audrey from Forget Street, but Edith was far more assertive. There were a few guys, too. There was Johnny, who had a big nose and was rather loud. Ron was one who always insisted on sitting in the corner no matter where we went. The drinking age was twenty-one back then, but we all had fake IDs and we girls wore quite a bit of makeup. My new girlfriends had shown me how to use makeup to look older and they loaned me sexy clothes so I wouldn't look so young. Even though I was only fourteen, my new friends and I went out as often as we could to bars, clubs, dances, whatever we could squeeze ourselves into. This was the era of jive dancing, and with so much time spent in the bars, we all considered ourselves jive-dancing experts. It soon became easy and not unusual for me to stay out all night. My mother was too far gone drinking to care, and Dad was easy to convince. I'd tell him I was sleeping at a girlfriend's house. He never doubted me.

On September 13, 1956, my mother announced once again that she was through drinking. She had just returned from a three-day binge and when she realized it was exactly one year since she had first joined AA, she decided to start her sobriety again on the exact same date. She asked us to sit down at the table. We obliged.

"You need to know," she gravely stated, "that you have an alcoholic living with you. But I have quit drinking."

Well, let the bells ring out and the banners fly, I thought. What was she talking about now? Nothing looked any different to me. Her clothes were all raggedy and her hair disheveled. And besides, she had quit so many times before. It was an old, broken record.

Mom explained that she met some people in Alcoholics Anonymous who had found a way to stay sober. She talked about how she humbly asked her Creator for help and so forth. Dad listened attentively. I was impatient and skeptical, but didn't say a word. I didn't want to make matters worse. When she finished announcing her latest resolution, my father gave her a long embrace and Mom went to wash up and get ready for bed. I wasn't impressed with this new story, and felt sorry for Dad, who still believed in and supported Mom.

A few weeks passed and Mom was still sober. I wasn't surprised yet, since she had quit many times before. A few months passed and she was still sober, and now that she was lucid and getting back to being a normal, functional wife and mother, my life started to be affected by it. She started dragging me to AA meetings where everyone was at least a hundred years old and there were slogans all over the walls that echoed lame clichés of encouragement. For a hardened teenager, it was as boring as it gets.

Dad tried to improve my life by enrolling me in the Miss Limoilou Carnival Beauty contest. It was great, actually. I came in first runner-up and gained a massive amount of attention. My picture was in the paper and I felt like a celebrity for about a week.

One Friday night in late January 1957, a few days before my fifteenth birthday, my friends and I snuck off to the Oyster Barrel, a nightclub where we often hung out on the weekends. Bill Haley and the Comets were playing there that night. This was a big deal. Bill Haley was a superstar in 1957 and I thought he was an amazing singer, not to mention handsome. I was really hoping I'd get the chance to meet him. We entered the dimly lit, smoky bar and the hat check girl gave us each a ticket stub which we were told to hang on to for a chance to win a bottle of champagne. I didn't pay much attention as I was preoccupied with the idea of meeting Bill Haley. I shoved the ticket in my coat pocket and scanned the bar. Hurrying to the counter, I ordered a White Bacardi and Coke, which I gulped down on the spot, enjoying the taste of rum and the warm feeling as it descended into my awaiting gut. I ordered a second right away, which I would sip meticulously for the rest of the evening.

We sat facing the stage, the dance floor to our right. I was sitting right in front of Bill Haley so if he looked up, he would see me twisting a lock of hair into a curl and making big, sappy doe eyes in his direction. As soon as the first song started, I grabbed Johnny by the arm and hauled him to the dance floor.

"All right!" Johnny bellowed. "Let's rock 'n' roll!"

With the enthusiasm of a motivational speaker, Johnny walked me to the dance floor and threw me to his arm's length, then started twisting and pulling and spinning me as though we were competing on American Bandstand. He kept screaming, "C'mon shake it, mama! Shake it!"

I was trying hard to be sexy as I danced, to get Bill Haley to notice me. I moved my hips sensually from side to side, but kept my eyes big and innocent. That way, I thought I was sexy without looking as if I were aware of it. I knew I had caught Bill Haley's attention with my hot dance moves, so during the band's break, my ego and I sat down and waited for Bill to come to my table. He didn't. I wasn't about to give up yet, though, so I danced through the entire next set with different guys, thus assuring Bill that I wasn't anybody's girl.

Johnny danced with Edith and Marylin alternately and at one point launched himself across the dance floor on his knees, screaming. Marylin and Edith ditched Johnny after that and danced with other guys as I was doing. On the next break, still no Bill Haley.

What a disappointment.

After another set, the MC got on the stage and announced that it was time for the big draw. Everyone got their ticket ready. I was looking for mine, but I had no idea where I had put it.

"Okay everyone," the MC enthusiastically announced, "this is for the bottle of champagne! Here goes!" He sank his hand into the great glass container that held all the tickets.

"Where in the hell did I put my ticket?" I yelled. I was rummaging through my stuff like a frantic tourist, spreading the contents of my bag on the table.

"Number one-two-seven," the MC spoke into the microphone. I found my ticket in my coat pocket just in time to hear the winning number. I looked at the number. I threw it down on the table, totally speechless. I had number one-two-seven!

"Number one-two-seven," the MC said again, this time even louder, causing a great deal of static to sound out of the speakers.

I jumped up from my chair and sat down again. I got up. I sat down. Up. Down. I must've looked like an idiot, yo-yoing like I was. Marylin grabbed my ticket, looked at it and yelled, "Over here!"

The MC pointed to our table and announced that I had won the champagne. It was the first time I ever won anything in my life. I collapsed on my chair. And then, to the astonishment of everyone, the bottle of champagne was delivered by none other than Bill Haley. Everybody lost their minds as though Jesus was delivering it.

"Congratulations!" he told me. "What's your name?"

"Thanks!" I said nervously and in awe. "Bobbi Priestson."

He shook my hand and kissed it. I looked at Marylin discreetly, certain that she wanted to kill me out of envy, but her mouth was hanging open. So was Edith's. Johnny was smiling profusely.

Bill put the champagne on the table and said, "Well ladies and gentleman, shall we have a drink, or shan't we?"

"Shall!" Marylin said.

"Yes! Shall!" I echoed.

"You're fucking right, shall!" went Johnny.

"Shall! Most definitely, shall!" said Edith.

Bill laughed and sat down with us.

"So Bill," said Johnny, as Bill was taking his seat, "what's it like to be a big-shot celebrity?"

"Jesus Christ, Johnny, shut up!" said Edith. "Terribly sorry, Mr. Haley."

"That's fine," Bill said. "It's a valid question."

"You see?" said Johnny. "It's a valid question."

"To be honest," said Bill, "it's nice to have people know who you are sometimes, but we work very hard. We're always either on the road, or writing, or recording and then there's the promoting. But I love my work." He turned to me. "So, Bobbi is it? What do you do? Are you a student?"

"Uh … yeah," I hesitated. I didn't want to reveal my age and get kicked out of the bar.

"We're in college!" Marylin said.

"Oh, really? What's your major?"

"Drinking!" Johnny said.

"We're studying business," Marylin corrected. "We all are." She nudged Johnny and told him to shut up.

"Wanna see my fake ID, Bill?"

"Johnny, will you shut the hell up?"

"That's okay, Johnny!" said Bill. "I'd love to see it."

Johnny pulled out his wallet and gave the phony ID to Bill. Bill examined it and commented, "Good work! Looks real as hell!"

"Thanks. You're okay, Bill. Fucking tops!"

Bill stayed with us for a solid twenty minutes and he was a very nice man. He was polite and well spoken, giving everyone a chance to talk. He really seemed to be listening, too. After a while, the MC got back on stage and announced that the champagne winner had won another surprise, and that was a dance with Bill Haley. Upon a signal from his band, who had returned to the stage, Bill turned to me, took my hand and said, "C'mon, Bobbi. Let's tear the floor up!"

My heart was racing and my palms were sweaty, I was trembling all over. Edith handed me her drink as a gesture of compassion and I grabbed and downed the whole thing. To this day, I have absolutely no knowledge of what was in the glass except that it was powerful. It hit the bottom of my stomach with a thud, having burned all the way down. The next thing I knew I was on the dance floor with Bill Haley, while the Comets played "Rock Around the Clock." The guitar player sang it since Bill was dancing with me. Bill flipped me over his hips and between his legs like a pro. I kept up really well, too. We put on quite a show for the Oyster Barrel. At the end of the song, Bill kissed my hand again and escorted me back to my table. "Let's hear it for Bobbi and Bill Haley, everyone!" the MC said.

Everyone cheered with great gusto, especially the girls. Bill went back on stage and I sank down on my chair, brimming with glee, convinced I was in love.

"Nice guy," said Johnny, taking a swill from his drink.

"Fucking tops!"

I have absolutely no recollection of how I got home or into my bed but I sure as heck remember waking up to the tune of my mother's shrill voice screeching at me as she yelled, "Bobbi, get up and get into the kitchen this minute!"

"It's Saturday, Mom. I want to sleep in," I answered groggily.

I looked at the clock and saw that it was nine o'clock. One minute passed. "Bobbi, into this kitchen, right now."

Another minute passed. I felt like I had an ice pick in my head and certainly didn't want to be bothered with whatever was the matter with her. Besides, hadn't she gone back to drinking yet, I wondered? Then I heard my father's voice thunder out.

"Young lady, you heard your mother. Get in here this instant!"

I knew I was in trouble if my father raised his voice. I staggered out to the kitchen and plopped down on one of the kitchen chairs and held on to my head to keep it from exploding. My father then, quite theatrically, threw a local newspaper down on the table. The paper was opened to the entertainment section, and there staring at us was a photograph of Bill Haley and me dancing, with the subtitle, 'Famous singer enjoys himself dancing with champagne winner.'

"Am I ever busted," I muttered under my breath.

"Tell me, exactly," Dad asked, "what is the meaning of this? And while I am at it, did you drink any of the champagne?"

"Drink champagne?" I asked, scandalized, my head throbbing. "No! I don't drink! Marylin brought us to the Oyster Barrel because Bill Haley was there and I didn't even want to go in the first place, but she kept insisting and stuff and well I don't have a car, so I just went along, but I only had a Coke. You know, that's Bill Haley!

He's the one who asked me to dance! It isn't my fault. Really!"
I was grounded for a month.

1 February 1957
Dear Diary,
My life was just improving when Mom had to go and
quit drinking and ruin it for me. I want to go out and see my
friends and dance all night. Mom doesn't miss a beat these
days. She's always either cleaning up or going off to some
meeting. Not to mention that she's dragged me to several of
these crappy meetings. On the brighter side, the apartment has
never looked better. At least there are no more potato peels on
the floor and Mom has taken to doing both Father's and my
laundry.
Bobbi

1 February 1957, evening
Dear Diary,
Big, big news! We're moving again. I can't believe it. I
heard Dad tell Mom that Valcartier has a brand new housing
complex and that there is definitely a place for us, which
means we're moving. I won't stand for this! Valcartier is an
army base!!! There's no way that I'm moving there, especially
on the verge of my fifteenth birthday.
Bobbi

2 February 1957
Dear Diary,
Mom has joined the army!!! What is this world coming
to?
Bobbi

4 February 1957
Dear Diary,
Well, it seems neither Mom nor Dad cares about what I have to say on the Valcartier issue. She told me to suck it up and to get used to the idea and that she wasn't going to let me get into all sorts of scrapes with the riff raff with whom I was used to going around. She said we're moving tomorrow. That's my birthday!
Bobbi

5 February 1957
Dear Diary,
Well this is just about the worst birthday one could imagine. My new home is in Valcartier, also known as the armpit of the universe. Nobody here has a clue about anything. Girls wear heels with bobby socks, for the love of God! I mean come on! I hate this place. I have to get up at 6 A.M. in order to get the bus to school and I can't participate in any after-school activities because the army bus that picks us up takes us home immediately after class is dismissed. Even the bus driver is a soldier and we can't get too cantankerous or we get a lecture from the colonel himself. To top it off, there's a curfew for all the teenagers. We all have to be home by 9 P.M. and if the Military Police sees any of us on the street, they pick us up and drive us home like a stray dog! My life is doomed. I will die a lonely old lady with no friends.
Bobbi

Chapter Seven

Living in the permanent married quarters of the Camp Valcartier army base could easily have been compared to being in prison. We lived in the officers' end of the military housing complex, which meant we had a house to ourselves. Lower ranking soldiers lived behind us in what was known as a duplex. Our house was something to behold. Its exterior was covered in bright pink shingles. It only had four rooms on the main floor, but it had a full basement for laundry and, eventually, a rec room. The kitchen was minute. The so-called table was only a leaf—just like what you would use to expand a regular table, but we had only the leaf part of it. One end of it was attached to the wall while one leg held up the other end. It was absolutely ridiculous.

When we saw the pink exterior, my father said that he was glad to be living in it and not across from it. Out of my bedroom window, I saw the back of officers' houses. My room was a disgusting mustard yellow, so disgusting that I covered its entirety, including the ceiling, with pictures of Elvis—who had become my idol since I didn't dare even think about Bill Haley without incurring my parents' wrath.

My fifteenth birthday party, on moving day, consisted of me, Dad and Mom. It was terrible.

"Make a wish," Mom said.

I wished she would start drinking again. I blew out the candles, ate a piece of cake and opened my present. "Hey. Look at that, a sweater."

"Try it on, honey," Mom said. I tried it on. "Oh my, you look just fine, Bobbi."

"Yep. That's a perfect fit, pumpkin," said my dad.

"Thanks."

As soon as they were out of sight, I was going to burn this piece of crap sweater. I finished my cake and asked to be excused, but Mom wanted to put on some music and dance. She said she knew how much I liked to dance.

I looked at the empty living room and felt so sorry for myself, I almost sobbed.

"Uh, no thanks. I think I'll just go to bed. I'm pretty tired."

"Well okay, Bobbi," she said. "I'm glad you like your sweater."

"Happy Birthday, sweetheart," said my dad, and kissed me on the forehead.

I went to my new room and sat on the bed, holding my sweater on my lap. A tear rolled down my cheek. I lay in bed, crying and confused. Now I was more than truly convinced that I was some kind of a mistake and that the Creator hated me.

Ever since she had quit drinking, Mom was developing this incredible indifference to my pouts. She was getting to be more and more like Meshomis, but she still had a ways to go before becoming as charming as him. Mom had gone from being totally oblivious to my existence to now telling me on a regular basis that I needed to 'suck it up.' She also got into the habit of saying, "Don't forget, Bobbi, that you're a V.I.P. and that God don't make no junk."

It was nice to hear that I was a very important person in my mother's eyes, and her attitude had improved a lot since she stopped drinking. In the back of my mind, though, I was sure she was just trying to manipulate me. I hadn't really got the hang of trusting her yet. "God don't make no junk" was something Meshomis said regularly, so I figured that in Mom's sobriety mode she was remembering what she had learned from her dad. I had mixed feelings about this whole situation. I sometimes felt like Mom was trying to show everyone she qualified for sainthood now that she was sober. Other times, I felt a softening in my heart for my blessed mother who had suffered so much in her life and now she was reassuring herself that the Creator loved her.

After moving to Camp Valcartier, I had to start a new high school. Boys and girls were segregated—unless you were considered brilliant, at which point you were sent to the overachieving mixed class. Girls wore a dark blue tunic that went down to the knees and white bobby socks that came up to the knees, as well as a long-sleeved white blouse. The only skin showing was your face, hands and knees.

I took my sweet time making new friends at the new school. It seemed like more trouble than anything else. School ran from eight-forty-five to three-forty-five. I hopped the bus at seven-fifteen and I got home at five-thirty. I had very little time to socialize at all.

Marylin, Edith, Johnny and I lost touch because there was really no more time for me to put into the friendship. We used to hang around after school at the corner store, but now while everybody else was hanging around enjoying themselves, I was stuck on the bus on my way to Valcartier. Nobody seemed to really care about me anymore, the way they had just earlier that year in my old high school. I had become the one on the outside looking in and I didn't like the situation at all. At first, the boys from the city still asked me out regularly but I wasn't allowed to go outside of Valcartier Camp unless my parents approved of my outing and of my company beforehand. After a while, the city boys just gave me up as a lost cause.

Most of my socializing took place on the bus ride to and from school. That isn't saying much, because I didn't care for the girls on the bus all that much and the driver was really strict. All I ever heard from the girls on the bus was condescending remarks about a girl's hair or a boy's buck teeth or how much of a loser he or she was, and so on. These were the same girls who wore bobby socks with heels! Molly Vantassel was the loudest and she and her cronies were insufferable. Molly was sixteen years old and had huge breasts, so she thought she owned the damn bus, and her grubby little fan club backed her up on all her vile commentaries. She worked her pals like a maestro, her breasts swinging left to right and up and down like a baton until they jarred, at which point Sergeant Riley, the bus driver, would bark at us, "You girls pipe down or I got a right mind to take you all to the colonel," and Molly's bouncing and jarring melons would settle down.

Molly's face lacked beauty. It was all about her breasts and a pink cashmere sweater that she wore over her uniform. Her cronies were all A- or B-size and they had gum stuck in their braces. Their skin was white and spotty. Molly had a boyfriend named Eddy who played hockey and was muscular. He also, apparently, had a huge penis. Molly said she'd never seen it, but she had felt it with her hands. Eddy was a man! She was a woman! She was going to show Eddy her big pink breasts this Friday night. He deserved it, she said.

If anyone on the bus, boy or girl, said anything nasty to her, she made sure you knew that Eddy would pay him a visit the next day and beat him up. She'd say, "Oh yeah? Well you'd better shut your fucking mouth or I swear to God, Eddy's gonna kick your ass!"

Eddy was big. Eddy played hockey. Her peers were impressed. Wow! How fantastic.

Also on the bus to school was this little waif called Paul Kack, who was the butt of many derogatory comments. He stood about five-foot-two, weighed about a hundred pounds soaking wet, and was rather homely looking. He had soft eyes that drooped like a St. Bernard's. I didn't think much of him at first and Molly and the gang often insulted him, commenting on how much of a dork he was. I sat next to Paul just to spite the others on the bus.

"Hey, can I sit here?" I asked.

"Uh, yeah, okay," he said, a little wary.

"I'm Bobbi. What's your name?"

"Paul Kack."

"Pleased to meet ya, Paul."

"Pleased to meet you too."

"You from Valcartier, Paul?"

"No, not really. I grew up in Ontario. My dad got transferred here."

"Yeah, me too. This place is the pits!" I said loudly enough for everyone on the bus to hear.

"No kidding."

He asked me where I was from and I gave him the long version: Lac LeVieux to Winnipeg to Petawawa to Montreal to Quebec City, and then here and there within the Quebec City area, and finally Valcartier Camp. He took a real interest in my story. He especially liked the fact that I was half Indian.

"You're Indian?" he asked, his eyes wide open.

"Yeah," I said, proud as hell.

"Wow! What tribe?"

"Ojibwa."

He sat there, anticipating more. I wanted to tell him a good Indian story, like a legend or something, but all I could think of at the moment was Meshomis killing chickens for supper and that wouldn't have been a very glorious story, I figured.

"Did you ever participate in a ceremony?" Paul asked.

"Of course! All the time!"

This was a bold lie. The truth was I had never participated in a ceremony other than with Meshomis, but I had to give him something, I thought. I started spinning tales about all the rituals and dances and magic that Indians are reputed to do. In my story, I was the one who lit the sacred fire and banged the drum and chanted the chants, and so on. Paul probably thought I was the chief of the tribe because I portrayed myself to be at the centre of all Indian activity.

"You're so lucky to be Indian," he told me. "I wish I were an Indian. I would go on the warpath and straighten out all these losers who live around here!" he bellowed, and started to laugh. He sure had a good sense of humour, I thought, being able to laugh at himself. And here I was lying about my heritage.

Paul and I became the best of friends. As the year passed, we became closer and closer. Paul was the first boy I ever befriended as an honest to God real friend. Looking back, I think he would have liked to get romantic, but he never made a pass at me and I'm glad he didn't because I was sure romance would ruin our friendship. Paul was nothing but respectful with me. My parents liked Paul so it was fine for me to see as much of him as I wanted, so long as my schoolwork was done.

Every day after school, once my homework was finished, I went out and around the neighbourhood and I'd meet Paul at the Teen Club before supper. I had an extra key to the place. We'd just meet for a few minutes because it was supposed to be out-of-bounds to us during the week. ·

My mother had started the Teen Club. She felt it was important for young people to have a place to let off steam and release pent-up frustrations by dancing. Man, that was a good move on her part. She harassed the colonel in charge of the army base until he gave us an old building to fix up and paint to our liking. We fixed the place up so that it looked like a beatnik's ballroom. We painted two walls orange and two walls purple, with colourful waves of yellow and red, then drew murals of stick people dancing on the waves. We hung big balls of dim lights all over the ceiling and we painted the cement floor black. Mom also scrounged old sofas and coffee tables from wherever and she convinced the army superiors to provide us with a jukebox filled with popular songs. The army base supplied us with free Coca-Cola and 7 Up.

We went dancing every Friday and Saturday night. The best part was our curfew was extended from nine p.m. to midnight. The downside was that we were chaperoned by parents and the military police, otherwise known as the Meatheads. They kept a watchful eye over our every move and searched each of us at least once a night to make sure we didn't smuggle in any alcohol.

When summer rolled in, Paul announced to me that he was going to go off and work for the hydro company in the far north for the whole summer.

"What in the world are you going to do there?" I asked.

"Cut trees, mostly."

"Cut trees?" I echoed, scandalized. I had seen Meshomis cut down many trees, but Meshomis was extremely strong. Paul was the size of a gerbil. I didn't have the heart to tell him that this tree cutting plan of his was going to be his end. I figured he'd be back, defeated, a week or so after he left. We said goodbye on June 25, the day after St. Jean Baptiste Day, a popular holiday for French Canadians.

Many days passed. I kept waiting for Paul to call and say he was back in town. I often asked my parents if they'd heard anything, but Paul hadn't called. Then one morning in August, I got a letter from him. I got really excited and ran to my room to read it. I jumped onto the bed, causing my stuffed animals to fall off, and tore open the envelope.

It read:
> July 13th 1958
> Dear Bobbi,
> How's my little one doin'? You better be behaving yourself because I'll be back soon. I sure don't like this place. It is cold and I do mean freezing and it's dangerous as hell too. Some summer! It's great exercise, but it's very dangerous. You got trees the size of skyscrapers falling every which way.
> Are you still as beautiful and as charming as ever? I'm sure you are. God knew what he was doing when he made you! I'll be back in a few weeks. Save me a seat on the bus (wink, wink). Take care, Bobbi.
> Your friend,
> Paul xox

Because the mail was so slow, Paul actually got back three days after I got his letter. I was standing on a stepladder hanging my laundry on the clothesline when he surprised me.

"Hey little one!"

I recognized his voice, turned around and saw a six-foot-three-inch, two-hundred-pound dude standing there, smiling at me and holding a present.

"Paul?" I asked, bewildered.

"The very one!" he said, all cool.

"Holy sufferin' succotash!" I said. "You're huge!"

"I know," he said, grinning. "I've doubled!"

I jumped down from the ladder and ran to give him a big, long hug, and he lifted me up and gave me the warmest hug back. He sure had shed his skinny little wimp image. We got caught up immediately, and he told me all about his job. I think I was still in shock because I kept interjecting with sentences like, "But Jesus, you're so damn big! I mean look at your arms!"

Paul would smile and say "Yeah, I know" and continue his story. I told him about my summer, which was boring as can be. The only noteworthy thing was how my cat Monster had gotten struck in the head with a dart. (He was okay.) For the rest of the summer we spent every minute that we could together.

School started, and Paul got an obscene amount of attention

from girls because he was so big and impressive now. Paul couldn't be bothered with them, though. These were the same girls who had laughed at him on the bus when he was scrawny and all of a sudden they were finding all sorts of reasons to talk to him. When Molly saw Paul, she went into a major phony-baloney reminiscence about how they went way back. She sat down on Paul's lap, uninvited, and practically shoved her big, fat breasts in his face and asked him what he'd been eating all summer.

"Get the hell off of me, Molly!"

He pushed her off and resumed talking with me. Molly got insulted and you could tell she was fuming, but she didn't make her usual threat. I think she and Eddy were broken up by that time, and besides, Paul could've torn Eddy to shreds had he felt so inclined. I smiled, proud of my friendship with Paul. It was funny, though, even though he was so handsome and we were best friends, we never dated each other. I absolutely adored Paul but only in a platonic way. He was like the brother I never had.

Around about this time, I met Jason Young. It was late September 1957, a beautiful, sunny, warm Saturday. The outdoor thermometer read seventy-six degrees so I decided to take advantage of the last warm days of the year and donned my bright yellow bikini. Before lying out in the sun, I took the time to admire myself in the mirror. I was impressed with the reflection looking back at me. My body was nicely tanned. My dark brown hair hung to my waist, and my big, dark brown eyes were framed with long black eyelashes.

"Yes!" I said to myself proudly. "I look good. A hundred percent Indian, baby!"

Within minutes after making myself comfortable on my lounge chair, a 1957 Triumph roared up the driveway, which impressed the hell out of me. Then my eyes roamed over to the breathtaking specimen of a man that was getting off the bike and walking over to me.

"Heeeey," he said in a deep voice. "Are you Bobbi?"

I felt slightly intimidated, but also felt that I should act tough. "Who wants to know?" I answered, as glibly as I could.

I was grateful I was wearing sunglasses so I could look him over inconspicuously. What a hunk he was to behold: six feet tall, broad shoulders under a tight-fitting yellow T-shirt, a black leather jacket and tight black jeans. He had pitch-black, curly hair, dark brown, complicated eyes, and full, sensual lips. Standing there somewhat aloofly, his weight shifted to one leg, he flashed me a well practiced smile à la Elvis and said, "I'm a friend of your boyfriend, Paul. He told me to meet him here because we're going riding together."

"Paul is supposed to be here in about an hour, but he didn't tell me to expect you. By the way, he's not my boyfriend. He's my best friend." I tried to keep from drooling all over myself. This boy was gorgeous!

"Well, that's good," he said, smiling shyly. "Do you have a boyfriend, then?"

"Actually, no I don't."

An uncomfortable pause followed, so I said, "Let's go for a short ride while we wait."

"Dressed like that?"

I looked myself over. Darn it. I had forgotten I was in my bikini. A little embarrassed, I said, "Of course not!" Then, regaining my coolest demeanour, I added, "Just give me a minute to get changed."

After our bike ride, we waited for Paul to arrive. In the meantime, we chatted about ourselves, and Jason asked me out for supper that evening. When Paul arrived, I took him aside and begged him to make their ride together short so that I could spend more time with Jason. Paul obliged.

That night I took the time to really get ready. I wore tight black jeans, a blue shirt and my black jacket. I arranged my hair in a ponytail because I assumed we'd ride to the restaurant on his motorcycle. He took me for a pizza in the city. Riding down the highway, I felt so special and sexy. To be with such a gorgeous man, who was so cool, was a great feeling. We had a great time, too, and we fooled around a little when he brought me back home.

Jason became the love of my life, and as each day passed, I fell in love with him with a deeper intensity. When I looked into his eyes, I saw that he loved me too. When we fooled around, Jason was really respectful about me not wanting to have sex. I was kind of hoping that he would ask me to marry him and then we would make love for the first time on our wedding night. It didn't matter to me that I was only fifteen. Hell, I was in love and I was almost sixteen. Besides that, I saw myself as a mature young lady who knew everything.

After a while, Jason began to be more and more persistent about sex. The only thing I permitted him to do was fondle my breasts through my top, and he wanted more. I never ever touched him. I had an aversion to touching him. I kept telling myself that I was going to caress his penis, but then memories of Gramps would flash in my mind and put me off. Eventually, I allowed him to see the top part of me undressed but that was as far as I was willing to go.

For a solid two years, Jason supported me in my beliefs about not having sex before marriage. Then he started becoming less and less attentive to me and sometimes I wouldn't see him for weeks at a time. I knew it was because I wouldn't put out. He was so special to me. I looked into his eyes and saw them so full of love for me. My body literally ached for him at times, but I wanted to wait until our wedding night. Although he was on the verge of turning nineteen, I was still just seventeen. By the time mid-December came around, just before my eighteenth birthday, I was getting fed up with not seeing him and I confronted him about it.

"Sweetheart," he responded, "I need to be honest with you. It's just too hard for me to be with you and not make love to you. It hurts me physically because I want you so much."

My bullshit detector went off at this point, but I ignored it. I should have stuck with my gut feeling, but when he looked at me with those big, brown eyes, I melted.

"Bobbi," he said, "when I am with you and we neck a bit, right away I get what the guys call lover's nuts. My balls … well … they get all swollen, red and sore. It gets so bad, I can barely walk. It's a terrible condition."

Good grief, the poor baby, I thought. Then Jason offered to show his balls to me.

"Thanks, but no thanks," I said quickly. "I believe you. I want you to understand that it affects me, too, Jason. Sometimes, I want you so badly I get a sore stomach. I get cramps just as bad as menstrual cramps!"

"Well," he responded, "at least you can take a couple of Midol and then you're fine. The only way I can get rid of the pain is to masturbate and believe me I don't want to ever do that. I want you, babe. I want to make love to you so that we become one." He put his hand on my heart and continued, "We are going to spend the rest of our lives together, sweetie, so what does it matter if we have sex now? You know we're going to get married."

I really didn't want to go all the way but I did not want to lose him, and it was looking like if I didn't put out, he would be gone. Just being around him was becoming exhausting to protect my virginity, because he was constantly trying to get into my pants with his hands and putting me on a guilt trip for not putting out. So, I decided that I would give myself to him as a Christmas present. When I presented this idea to him he was thrilled. He told me he would make all the arrangements. I assumed that he was going to rent a hotel room with wine and cheese and all the rest of it.

As I drifted off to sleep, I imagined the perfect scenario for our first love-making experience. I had bought myself a long silky negligee as part of my trousseau, which I kept in my cedar chest. I saw myself coming out of the hotel bathroom wearing my beautiful sheer white gown. Jason would be standing there waiting for me, wearing a smoking jacket, and he would scoop me up in his arms and lay me on a bed covered with rose petals. I saw us feeding each other fresh strawberries dipped in melted chocolate, followed with tender words and sensual touches, which would lead to an explosive passion, just like in the movies.

Two days before Christmas, Jason, the love of my life, phoned to tell me that he had arranged everything for Christmas Eve. He said we were going to spend the whole night together.

"You'll need to come up with some excuse for your parents so that you can stay all night, okay?"

I knew that wouldn't be a problem because the 24th was my parents' anniversary. Ever since Mom had stopped drinking, the two of them were always lovey-dovey and I was sure they would appreciate having me out of their hair so they could have a romantic evening together. Sure enough, they fell for my story about a bunch of us gals having a pyjama party.

It seemed like forever before it was time to meet my love. I tried out ten different hairdos. I was so nervous, but I kept reassuring myself that everything would be all right. I carefully packed my negligee along with all my toiletries, including my Avon perfume called Tender Trap, and off I went to the park, where we had agreed to meet.

Jason picked me up as planned, and then drove us straight to the house of Brian Gauthier, one of his friends.

"What are we doing here?" I asked.

"Hey, princess, Brian's parents are gone for the whole night and Brian said we could use his bedroom for a few hours. He's going out partying. Isn't this just so cool?"

"Uh, well, this isn't exactly what I had in mind," I stammered as my heart broke. Then I continued, worried, "Jason, did you tell Brian that we were going to make love?"

"Of course I did! All the kids are doing it nowadays. It is just you that's a holdout."

I looked at him and Jason could tell by the expression on my face that I was about to cry.

"Bobbi," he said, softening his voice, "I would love to be able to take you to a nice hotel and go for the whole works, but I just can't afford to. You know that I've just joined the army and am off to Kingston in a couple of weeks. We won't see each other for weeks at a time. Let's just go on with the plan for tonight and I promise, one day, I'll make it up to you. We'll go to Niagara Falls for our honeymoon or something!" He smiled and took me in his arms.

I was hesitant but as Jason comforted me and told me how much he loved me, I tearfully agreed.

Big Mistake.

As soon as we got into the house, we were greeted by Brian, who had been waiting for us to arrive before he could leave.

"Hey," he said, leering at me. "Jason, I never thought you would ever get 'Little Miss Bobbi' to bed. Well, stranger things have happened, I guess. Have fun, you two!" Brian sauntered out of the house.

I was totally mortified. This was certainly not turning out as planned. I took my overnight bag and started heading to the bathroom to change into my negligee. I thought at least this part of the evening wouldn't be ruined. Jason grabbed me by the arm.

"Where are you going?" he asked. "Let's not waste any time."

"I want to change into my negligee," I shyly contested.

"As I said before, baby, let's not waste any more time. Besides, I want to undress you."

Before I could say anything, he took my bag from me, tossed it away from us and led me into Brian's room. He found his way in the dark to the night stand, where he turned on the bedside lamp. I looked around the room. It was painted pea green and had a yellow ceiling. The bed hadn't been made, and right in the middle of the room was a hockey bag, from which was emanating a strong stench of sweaty clothing and stinky socks. Before I could comment, Jason started to slowly undress me. I didn't know what to do, so I stood there feeling like a dummy while he stripped me bare. As soon as I was naked, I disappeared under the blankets of Brian's unmade bed and covered myself up to my chin as Jason stripped to his hairy, bare ass. He dived into bed penis first and started groping me. He got right on top and kissed me a couple of times, then reached down and took his erect penis and manipulated it until he got the tip of it into the entrance of my vagina then pushed it in steadily and strongly.

"Yikes! Ouch! Jesus! Take it easy! Ouch … wait a second!"

"Oh yeah, baby, yeah!"

"Ouch! Ouch!"

By the time I finished swearing about the pain, it was all over.

"That was completely gross!" I announced. "Horrible!"

"Babe, of course it happened fast. After all, I have been waiting years to make you mine. The next time will be better."

Next time, my ass! We lay back in the bed and Jason started to tell me all about how he made the pass that led to the winning goal during his last hockey game. He explained how this really good player on the opposing team had the puck and was on the attack. But Jason somehow maneuvered the puck away from him and stealthily passed it over to his teammate who one-timed it right into the goal. It sounded so exciting. And I fell in love with him again. We started to kiss softly but it almost immediately turned to necking and fondling. It seemed like only minutes had passed and Jason was ready for more action. The second time was just as fast and just as mechanical as the first. As soon as he was done, I got out of bed and had a shower. I felt like I needed to scrub myself raw.

In the shower, I vowed to myself that I wasn't going to participate anymore in this charade of love-making. I guess Jason must have sensed my disappointment because by the time I got out of the shower, he had raided the bar and had prepared me a strong Bacardi and Coke. I followed it with a second drink, which resulted in my becoming willing to have sex one more time.

After the disappointing third experience, I ran to the bathroom to wash myself again. Neither one of us really knew what we were doing, frankly. I didn't know about sexual enjoyment and all Jason could think about was ejaculation.

After we had sex three times, I told Jason that this was definitely too gross to continue.

Six weeks later, on my eighteenth birthday, I tested positive. Happy Birthday. I was pregnant. Holy Jesus, I thought. I mean really! All of my friends had been making out for years and nobody had gotten pregnant. I told Jason that I was going to have his child.

He told me that he had fallen in love with someone else. He said that he would marry me, but that he didn't love me anymore.

My disappointment turned suddenly to anger. "Yeah, well here's a news flash, buddy," I screamed at him. "I will never marry you just to have it thrown in my face later that you had to marry me. Forget it and forget me, you son of a bitch."

Chapter Eight

Discovering I was pregnant was a wake-up call for me. No doubt my new awareness of life's events could have been used in a positive way but I didn't see it that way. I fed my self-pity and feelings of being unloved, all the while knowing that I was being given the wonderful gift of a new life. I knew that I would have to become even more devious than I had been in the past. I knew that I had to hide my pregnancy as long as possible but I also knew that I was going to need a lot of support.

Fortunately, I suffered from no morning sickness so I was able to hide my condition until I was six months along. The only person I told, other than Jason, was Paul, who was in Kingston doing his last semester at a one-year college course. Looking back now, I realize I certainly gave him one hell of a shock with my news. He had believed all along that I hadn't slept with Jason so I felt no need to confess when the hideous act occurred. However, upon learning of my pregnancy and Jason's rejection, I made a quick trip to Kingston and tracked him down. If he wondered what I was doing in his neck of the woods, he didn't ask. I told him that I wanted to treat him to a movie. The name of the movie was *Three Coins in a Fountain*, a story about three young girls, one of whom becomes pregnant. When we got to the part where the pregnant girl tells her friends she is pregnant, I leaned over to Paul and whispered, "So am I."

The next thing I knew, he had grabbed me and marched me right out of the theatre. When we got to the sidewalk, he spun me around and yelled, "How did you do that?"

"Well now," I meekly answered, "do you really want me to explain?"

"No, no, damn it, no. But now what are you going to do?"

I started to cry as I answered that I had no idea what to do. All I knew was that I would be labeled easy and I knew I wasn't. Paul took me to a nearby restaurant and reassured me that he would be there for me and not to worry. He went on to say that he was willing to marry me to give the baby a name. I cried even harder. You see, in those days, being an unwed mother was most certainly not the thing to do. I knew Paul's idea was a good solution but I knew that he deserved better than to be trapped into a marriage with someone who didn't love him in that way. Not only that, I thought, I absolutely, positively, hated the sex act. He consoled me by telling me he would be back in Quebec in May and would be there for me in whatever decision I made.

When I was six months along, I finally told Mom about my condition. I had been wearing a tight girdle to hide my pregnancy and it was just too painful to continue this torture. She was scandalized and appeared to be more worried about her social status being affected than my well-being. She stated in no uncertain terms how I had disgraced the family name.

"Bobbi, how could you do this to us? What did we do to deserve this kind of treatment from our only child? You must never tell your father and you have to give the baby up. There, that will make everything okay. I'll contact a place that houses people like you. When the baby comes, you will give it up, return here and nobody will be the wiser." She rattled this out all in one breath and then heaved a sigh of relief when she realized she had fixed the problem.

"Bobbi, you have to understand that you cannot, I repeat cannot keep this baby. It's illegitimate. Illegitimate! Don't you see? Your father would be devastated and destroyed. Be reasonable, Bobbi. Be reasonable, for God's sake."

I can barely express how I felt. What the hell? Had she not been raised by the same wonderful man, Meshomis, who often told me what a blessing having a child was? Honestly, I wanted to die. I thought Mom was right about not keeping the baby but only because I didn't want to hurt my father. I listened hard to Mom, but

I knew I couldn't comply. I just couldn't do it. I definitely wanted to keep my child. I loved that little being moving around in my tummy. I was scared and confused. I didn't know what to think. However, I agreed to continue to hide my pregnancy, so off I went to a home for unwed mothers in Montreal. I was a skinny, pregnant, heartbroken girl, rejected by her boyfriend as well as her mother.

The home I was sent to was an annex to a hospital run by Christians. Every morning following breakfast and general cleanup duties, we had a couple of hours of forced free labour to do. This involved placing ink cartridges into pen holders. Each of us had to complete two thousand pens before lunch.

After a meager lunch, the residents who had participated in singing hymns at the church service the previous evening were allowed to have the rest of the day off. I refused to be a part of anything to do with church. I didn't feel particularly religious. As a matter of fact, I was furious with the Creator for allowing me to get myself in this situation. I felt that I had been completely abandoned by the Great Spirit. I did not want to partake in useless prayers, nor did I have any interest whatsoever in singing praises to a god who had abandoned me. Because of my attitude, I was obliged to work as janitorial staff for the attached hospital, every afternoon.

I was washing four flights of stairs in the hospital on my hands and knees the day my labour began. I knew absolutely nothing about childbirth. I had no idea how babies entered the world, literally. I didn't know how they made their grand entrance and had been too shy to ask anyone. However, it wasn't difficult for me to recognize that the pain I was in was due to the beginning of labour. I told a staff member, who rushed me to the hospital and stayed with me until I was registered. This all happened around four in the afternoon. The contractions were not unbearable until seven that evening. I asked for some kind of pain relief. To this day, I can still see and hear the reply I got. A beautiful, saintly and serene-looking nurse came into my room with a wondrous smile on her face.

"How can I help you, my dear?" she asked in a soft musical voice.

"I really need something to ease this pain," I replied, trying to mimic her voice.

She picked up my chart and became aware that I was an unwed

mother. She transformed into an ugly ogre and with the voice of a horrible monster screeched at me, "You don't deserve anything to help you out. You are nothing but a common tramp. You deserve all the pain you get, so don't bother me anymore. Do you understand me?"

I lay back on my bed, covered myself with my blankets and began whimpering in pain. The nurse looked at me with all the disdain she could muster and calmly announced, "Maybe, from now on, you will think twice before you leap in and out of men's beds. Maybe you will stop being a slut." Then she turned around and walked out.

It took me some time to absorb the cruel words she had thrown my way. The pain was excruciating and I became hysterical. I staggered out to the hall and started yelling and hollering, disturbing every patient in the vicinity until finally the doctors grabbed me, hauled me back to my bed, tied me down and knocked me out.

I was still asleep when Phyllis was born, but then the nurses shook me awake and she was placed in my arms. A staff member from the home came to me saying, "Look at this beautiful child you have given birth to. I know you love her but guess what?"

I listened in innocence and in relief from the prior agony.

"In five days," the nurse added, "you are going to give her up for adoption because you are a sinner and are unworthy of being her mother. She deserves better than an immoral mother."

I looked her square in the eye and answered with every particle of strength left in me, "Over my dead body. Nobody will take my child away from me."

I stuck to my guns and refused to sign adoption papers. My child was placed in a foster home in Montreal and within five days of her birth, I was back in Quebec City going to business college. I was determined to get an education so that I could support my child. Paul was there and supported me as a friend. He collected baby clothes for me and took me to Montreal to see my child every second weekend.

I developed a good relationship with Phyllis's foster parents who absolutely adored my daughter. They were kind, loving and supportive. When the Children's Aid Society decided to put my child up for adoption without my permission, the foster family contacted me and warned me what was about to happen. Paul and I went to Montreal right away and, with the foster parents' awareness and permission, we brought Phyllis to Quebec City. I didn't know where I would place her because Dad still didn't know about her, and I was still living at home with my parents. I placed her in an emergency placement setting until one of Paul's friends came up with a group-home for foster children and I placed her there, where she lived until I married two years later.

I finished college and got a good job with the Bank of Montreal. Every day after work as well as Saturdays and Sundays, I faithfully went to see my child. But something had happened inwardly with me. I put all of Meshomis's teachings on the shelf and developed a mean streak. I was full of hate and anger. I started to get into drugs and alcohol again because without these crutches, my conscience wouldn't allow me to be so nasty.

I was a hard-working young lady and I excelled in my work. I considered myself a good mother, given the circumstances. Other than that, though, every evening I partied a lot. I developed a goal— to 'get them before they get me.' I had no idea what my philosophy meant, but I knew I was out to get even for what had happened to me. I developed many masks that I used in what I considered the appropriate situations. I had absolutely no respect for most of the male species and delighted in hurting guys who cared for me—other than Paul, who always remained a true friend. I assumed all men were on the make and my place was to get even with them, especially if they hurt one of my girlfriends.

I enjoyed playing the role of Little Miss Innocent Bitch. She really captured men's hearts. She sought and destroyed males, so to speak, before they had any idea of what was going on. I used her to get revenge for any of my girlfriends who'd been dumped by some son of a bitch they cared for.

For example, when I was nineteen, my good friend Diane phoned me one day to moan and cry hysterically that her boyfriend, Brian, had split up with her. He told her the reason was that she was too serious about him. Brian was the one who had given Jason his home to seduce me. I had vowed revenge then, and here was my opportunity. He was a real bastard. He had told Diane that they would get married just to get into her pants and then, with the mission accomplished, he told her she was too serious. This situation sent a rage through me. I felt it from my toes all the way to my head. I was fire. It felt like a volcano about to erupt.

Preparing revenge was sweet.

Here was the plan. What I would do was to calm down, call Brian and make a date with him. He'd be like, 'Uh okay, Bobbi, uh, where do you wanna go?' Then when we were out dancing together, I'd knee him in the balls like a fire truck and break him down to size. Yes! That was what I'd do. Anyhow, Brian was such an imbecile. I never knew what Diane saw in him. Diane was such a loser with guys. She believed everything they said. Absolutely everything.

I called Brian. "Hey, how's it going?" I asked him.

"Great!" he answered.

"Diane called a while ago to say that you broke up with her."

"Yes. It's one of those things, you know?"

"Uh-huh," I grunted.

"Uh-huh?"

"I want to know if you are interested in anyone else."

"Not exactly, no. Why do you ask?"

"Well ... you know ... I thought ..." Come on, you big stupid idiot, ask me out!

"Maybe you and me could go out sometime ... eh, Bobbi? What do you think?"

"Yes, that would be great," I said sweetly.

He was so dense you could make him roll over and play dead. As I lied to this jerk, I saw myself roasting in hell forever as punishment for setting him up. Even though I was capable of vicious things I still wholeheartedly believed in Heaven and Hell, but I figured at this point in my life I was going to go to Hell no matter what. And this was well worth it, to get revenge for Diane. After Einstein asked me out, we made a date for the next night.

What Brian saw when he picked me up was an innocent little kitten. I was dressed sophisticated yet sexy. I wore a tight skirt and heels and had shaved my legs to make them like vanilla. I wore a pink cashmere turtleneck sweater, which made my breasts round like melons and soft like my legs. When I opened the door to greet Brian, I leaned forward and kissed his cheek and made a little sigh as if to imply that my greatest dream was in front of me. He's such an idiot, I thought. We went to Les Vieux Canons, a very posh restaurant in downtown Quebec City with terrific food.

Even though Brian was an idiot about relationships, you had to hand it to him, he knew his way around town. We had their lobster special. As I pulled the lobster apart, I compared the lobster's fate to how Brian was going to feel when I was finished with him. I purred like a kitten and gave his boring stories my full attention. I really built up the bastard's ego. I'd flash and bat my eyes at him and look so interested in what he was saying. After our meal, I convinced Einstein to go dancing. I chose a romantic little piano bar downtown called the Clarendon, where the band played slow romantic music. We had a booth in the corner near the emergency exit. My plan had to be well-timed if I didn't want to end up arrested. Once seated, I excused myself and went and called a cab. I told the dispatcher that the driver should arrive in exactly fifteen minutes at the Clarendon, on the side street where I would be.

"Not the front door!" I told him.

"Yes, Madame," he said without a care. He couldn't have cared less if I asked the driver to pick me up in a crack alley. That worried me a little. If the cab wasn't there, it would be risky. Cab drivers, they don't care about anything. I then spoke to the lead piano player, Joel, and requested that he play the song "Last Date" and that it be the third song coming up. He agreed. He seemed charmed. He had no idea what I was up to either. No one in the Clarendon had any idea. Ha! Were they in for a surprise. I figured each song lasted about three minutes and that between songs Joel would take about a minute or two to announce the name of the next song and to keep the crowd warm. I'm somewhat of a perfectionist when it comes to revenge. I then came back to the booth, sat down and snuggled up to Brian.

"Let's dance," I said.

He looked at me and said, "Uh, okay." He didn't look very sure of himself.

I managed to finish the first dance without incident. Einstein and I stayed on the dance floor as Joel announced the next song.

"Oh Brian," I whispered. "Let's dance again. Please."

During the second song, I whispered that I was really enjoying dancing with him. Ha! If he only knew that I was going to knee him in the balls like a freight train. I ran my fingers through the back of his hair and lightly pressed my breasts against his chest—just lightly though because I didn't want him to mess up my cashmere sweater. Finally, "Last Date" started. I got a pang of nervousness and for a brief second thought about forgetting the whole thing. Diane was an idiot. She should have known better not to sleep around with someone like Brian the imbecile. Right then Brian looked at me and said, "Hey I love this song." What an idiot. The plan was back on.

"Me too," I said and stepped back from him, sweetly smiled like a cute little kitten and then bam! I slammed my right knee into his crotch like a hurricane. Kaboooooooom!

"Uuuuuuuuuuuuuuggggghhh," he groaned and crumpled to the ground, like a sandcastle, in agony. I gave him a look implying he was pure evil and I was hoping to exorcise this demon and said, "Screw you Brian, you son of a bitch!"

I ran out the emergency exit, hopped into my cab—which was there, thank God—and took off. Mission accomplished.

Another one of the 'characters' I played in the bar scene was the Pretty Little Princess Bitch, in need of being saved from the cruel world. I used her when I was 'cruising' alone and didn't want any trouble. I dressed in lightly coloured dresses with a flared skirt. I wore three or four crinolines under the skirt, which made it stand out stiffly and gave me an illusion of innocence, especially with a trace of lace barely showing at the bottom. I wore my waist-length hair in one thick ponytail tied back in a red or blue ribbon, or sometimes in two sexy pigtails, one on each side of my head. I wore my bangs past my brow to emphasize my big brown eyes. I wore just a dab of makeup, but I paid special attention to my eye makeup to make my eyes look innocent and doe-like.

I would go to Bal Tabarin for the night and sit on the bar stool pretending to be misplaced and uncomfortable. One time, I watched this gorgeous specimen of man on the dance floor. He definitely had moves and rhythm, and I loved dancing. He caught me looking, so I demurely looked away. After the song was over, he came over to speak to me. He had a great tan, he really did. He was fair-haired with blue eyes. He had on a tight white short-sleeved shirt that showed off his muscles. He wore tight blue jeans that moulded his slim hips. I tried not to hang my tongue out like a St. Bernard.

Unfortunately, Drew, which turned out to be his name, came up with some loser-line and I had to hold back my disgust. One needed to be charming, not simply good-looking. I can't even remember what he said exactly, something about being Drew and he was here to protect me, except he said it so that Drew rhymed with the word 'you.'

"Well hello, Drew," I responded. "Are you going to put those muscles to good use and keep the bad guys away from me tonight?" At least I had some charm, I thought, with my clever line. I tilted my head slightly to the side as I looked up at him with my big doe eyes. My evening of fun began. We danced all night. Drew treated me with a great deal of respect. I could see the wheels turning in his head. He was planning to play it slowly. In the early hours of the morning, after dancing with him for about three hours, he thought he was certainly taking me home and at least getting to first or second base. I excused myself to go to the ladies' room and went home instead. Take that. I wasn't going to give him the satisfaction. That's what Little Princess Bitch was like.

Another favourite character of mine was the Tough Little Bitch. I loved it when I knew I would be escorted for the evening by one of my male buddies as my protector, especially when it was Paul. Paul was even taller and more muscular than he had been in school and he still thought I was the best thing that was ever born. After he filled out his little waif's body, he started getting a lot of attention from girls. But he never forgot how he had been treated before. He wanted nothing to do with those other girls. I was his best friend. He called me 'little one' all the time, which really made me feel special. We adored each other, but our relationship remained strictly platonic. We never even kissed. He may as well have been my big brother. I sure didn't want to complicate or ruin our relationship with romance. That would be trouble.

When I'd go out with Paul to a club, I could really be tough and threatening to anyone I wanted. I started fights and Paul would finish them! I became the Tough Little Bitch that nobody better mess with if they knew what was good for them. Even though I was a tiny little thing, I always believed that my roar was that of a lion and that people better just step away.

Paul often asked in amazement, "Little one, why do you act like this?" His eyes displayed confusion. Paul didn't really want to be fighting but he wasn't going to let anyone talk to me without respect either, even if I started all sorts of trouble. "Why do you pretend that you're mean?"

I really didn't have an honest answer for him. I just knew that I had to 'get them before they get me.' I had to get them. The answers came later—much later.

The downside to all this role-playing was I didn't like myself at all. I became extremely cynical and found myself withdrawing from the world. My masks became my life. I presented an image of a superior high-class snob, but nobody knew how I really felt. I hated myself. I started to believe I was evil and deserved nothing good in life. I turned more and more to using soft drugs to be able to cope. I refused to let down my defences. That is to say, until I met Gary.

Chapter Nine

I met Gary on a beautiful autumn day in the fall of 1961. I was living at Camp Valcartier army base with my parents. Camp Valcartier, just north of Quebec City, was so beautiful in the fall. Everywhere I looked, the leaves of the maples and birches were stretching in full exposure, their intense fire reds and sunshine yellows mixed in with their sunset oranges, contrasting with the dark green of the firs. The Creator was showing us that there was no reason to fear death because the leaves were incredibly beautiful, even though they would soon be falling to the hardening ground.

I was nineteen years old. I had finished college, was living with my parents and had a good job working for the Bank of Montreal. I drove to the post office to pick up my parents' mail for them. I went into the tiny little building that held row upon row of mail boxes. I opened ours, found no mail, relocked it and headed to the exit. As I reached to open the door, someone coming in opened it for me. There stood the most gorgeous human being I had ever seen in my life. He still had one foot on the top step leading to the door, which put us at the same eye level. And his eyes made me weak at the knees. They were sea green with a natural black outline, framed with a double layer of long black eyelashes. Curly blond hair was sneaking out of his army hat. Covering his little pug nose were the cutest little square freckles that I had ever seen. I was mesmerized. I couldn't move. His smile lit up his whole face. He leaned back a little and pushed his army hat back. "Well now, just look at what the Good Lord has put in my path," he said.

His voice alarmed me. I didn't know why, but I knew I had to get away from this man before I fell into something I could never get out of. "If you have finished gawking at me," I snapped, "will you move so I can leave?" The poor man looked taken aback by my rudeness.

"Now I remember you," he said, before moving out of my way.

Not believing him, I charged out and ran to my car before he could say more. My body was so hot, I was melting. Hormones were galloping at breakneck speed. My only thought was to get out of there, to drive fast and escape these feelings I had thought were gone forever. I had never felt so rattled. I was terrified. I thought I was going crazy. How stupid can a person be, going totally weak at the knees because someone says hi? I sat in my car shaking too much to get the key into the ignition.

As I sat trembling in the car, I slowly recalled that I had met this fascinating, sexy individual before—not just once, but twice. The first time was in the summer of 1957 when I was fifteen, living on this same army base with my parents. Someone had fired a small dart into my cat's forehead. The dart hadn't stayed in the wound but still, Monster's head was bleeding. I loved my cat and I didn't know what to do. There wasn't any veterinarian nearby so I took him to the military hospital. I fell to my knees in front of the first soldier I saw, a young medic. "Please help fix my cat," I begged. "Please, please fix Monster for me."

The young soldier had leaned back a little and pushed his army hat back and said, "Well now, just look at what the Good Lord has put in my path."

Same actions, same person. It had been him, and he had just said that he remembered me. I had been too worried about Monster at the time to pay attention to him, but I did remember his gentle tone of voice when he talked to me. "Come here, little girl," he had said, as if he were talking to a child. "I'll fix your cat for you and it won't even hurt him."

I had admired his gentleness as he applied disinfectant to the wound. Because of his kindness, I decided not to yell at him for calling me a little girl. And anyway, I was grateful for his help.

The second time I had seen this good-looking man was on New Year's Eve of 1959 when I was seventeen years old. He was at my friend Suzanne's party. I didn't pay much attention to him, as I wasn't very fond of men at the time. At some point during the party he came up and talked to me, mistaking me for someone else. "What are you doing back here, little girl?" he asked. I looked at him like he was crazy. What did he mean 'back here'? I decided he must be drunk.

"Little girl," he continued, "I just took you home. You had better skedaddle out of here. We don't need a babysitter anymore. All the adults are here now. You should go home and get to bed."

Suzanne interrupted him, "Gary, this isn't the babysitter. I have to admit she looks a lot like her, though."

I felt sudden anger. I knew the babysitter, and she was only thirteen years old! I looked at Gary and said, as pleasantly as I could, "You are a self-centred son of a bitch." After that, I had done my best to forget this guy. I was scared by how he was capable of getting under my skin so easily. Now he had shown up in my life for the third time.

A light knock on the car window jarred me back from my memories. I looked up and there was Gary, smiling sweetly at me. I looked down at the steering wheel and rolled down the window.

"What do you want?" I managed to whisper, amazed that my voice didn't come out sounding like a shrew.

"I bet your daddy doesn't know you have taken his car," he said, sweetly. He reached through the window and caressed my sweaty hand. "You had better get it home right away before you get caught. If your daddy doesn't catch you, maybe the Military Police will, and then you will be in big trouble."

"What the hell are you talking about?" I yelled, flaring into anger, just like the last time. "This is my car and I can drive it when and where I want to, so just screw off." I glared at him.

He looked taken aback, but my temper helped me to forget my wobbly knees and weak elbows. I started my car and drove away. I felt sure I had seen the last of him and I convinced myself I never wanted to see him again. However, I took the time to find out his full name, Gary Wendall, and that he was a soldier in the Medical Corps and he was from St. John's, Newfoundland.

I also found out that he was ten months older than me and that his birthday was April 13.

I decided to forget about this gorgeous jerk and get on with my dreary life. I moped around Camp Valcartier, sullenly. I felt as a jigsaw puzzle would: a mess, pieces scattered and confused. I was a young single mother hiding her child in a foster home because of the stigma attached to the situation. Being a single mother in 1961 was an unbelievably scandalous state of affairs, and Mom and I were definitely not on the same footing. She was always on my case about giving up the baby. "Mom," I used to answer her, "get one thing straight, I will never give up my baby. Never. Never. Never."

I wished things were different, that the past wasn't there, but it was and there was nothing I could do to change it. I wanted to be myself, unabridged without hiding or running, but I was scattered and lost. I was fear and fear was me. Flashbacks to spiritual lessons I received as a child used to come back to me but I was too confused at the time to apply them. "Fear, Angekwe, makes us good runners on the Black Path," Meshomis had said. "Fear stands for 'Forget Everything And Run.' We run away because of fear. I don't run, Angekwe, but I want to sometimes. Fear can also mean 'Face Everything And Recover.' It is much better to walk on this Red Path."

My feelings seemed part of a mud puddle, too murky to recognize. I now firmly believed nice folks finished last. I was scared to take down the walls consisting of my many fears. I was afraid to trust anyone. After all, the father of my baby had used me, and then rejected me when I became pregnant. Mom had sent me away alone to have my baby so she wouldn't be looked upon as a bad mother and so I wouldn't be ridiculed. She still hadn't permitted me to tell Dad about my baby because she was still hoping I would give her up for adoption. At the Home for Unwed Mothers, I had been ridiculed for not being willing to pray the 'White Man's way.' I was lonely, so very lonely. But I was also sick of getting hurt every time I let down my guard. The word 'fear' ate at me. Fear of rejection, fear of being ridiculed, fear of being alone, just to name a few. It seemed to take over my personal power.

A couple of weeks after running into Gary at the post office, hoping that I could do something to change my negative attitude, I decided to spend the weekend in the city with my girlfriend Verna. Her place was in Quebec City, on St. Marie Street, right uptown within the city walls. Verna had very little money. Her tiny bachelor pad consisted of a small, scarcely furnished living room and kitchen area which held an aluminum table with an orange flowery surface and two wooden chairs that did not match the table. There was a small bathroom in which the sink and toilet almost touched. Her bedroom could only hold a single bed. When I visited, Verna would take her mattress off and put it in the living room. I would sleep on it while Verna would sleep on the box spring in her room.

I was sprawled out on my bed in the living room when the phone rang. It was Verna's boyfriend, Joey. He told her that one of his friends was with him and he was wondering if Verna could fix up a blind date for this guy, so they could double date.

"Bobbi, do you fancy going out on a double date?" she asked.

Since having the baby, I had had a negative attitude towards men. I had concluded there was no room in my life for a man. They would only be after sex anyway.

"If I can't get my own date, I will remain dateless," I replied. "There is no way I would go out with a stranger."

"She says she will never go out with a stranger," she relayed. Verna's next sentence shocked me into moving faster than I had ever moved in my life. "It's with a guy named Gary Wendall. He ran into you at the post office and really wants to meet you." I was off my bed, showered, dressed and ready to go before Verna got off the phone.

We had to wait a half-hour before Joey and Gary showed up. Meanwhile, we moved my mattress back to Verna's room. I paced up and down the tiny floor space. Every couple of minutes, I changed my mind about going with Gary. Finally the doorbell rang. I flew to the door and opened it. There was Gary, my Adonis. Even though it was late fall, his hair was still sun-streaked blond with a little curl that fell to his right eye. His denim jacket was casually thrown over his arm. He had on a tight, pale blue T-shirt. His jeans hugged his thighs, moulding his strong muscular legs. He had broad, well-developed shoulders and a thick back that funneled into a narrow tight waist. His chest was composed of two thick, carved slabs of pectoral muscles which rippled under his t-shirt. I had to conquer this man, I thought.

I glanced at him from top to bottom, put on my demure role, and sweetly said, "I guess the first thing I should do is apologize for being so rude to you at the post office." I expected him to say it wasn't necessary.

"Yes, I agree with you," he surprised me by teasing. "I certainly do deserve an apology. After all, I thought you were driving a stolen car."

Now what was I going to say? We locked eyes. Then we both smirked at the same time and collapsed with laughter as we remembered our last meeting. It looked like we were finally off to a good start. However, I still didn't understand why I was so rattled in this man's presence. We started on our way to the Chateau Frontenac, a posh place in the upper section of Quebec City where we planned to dine.

Joey was driving, so Gary and I got into the back seat. As soon as we got in, Gary grabbed me and tried to kiss me. I thought he was going to maul me. I got unbelievably angry but I didn't want to ruin the evening for the other couple, so I whispered angrily, "You son of a bitch. Where do you get off thinking that you will even get to kiss me on the cheek? You invited me out for supper and I am hungry. Do you get it? You will be polite and behave like a gentleman and we will pretend we are having a good time. Have you got that, you low-life?"

He looked at me for a moment and then answered with a sentence that confused me. "Young lady, I have every intention of marrying you."

Calling him by his last name, I scoffed, "Wendall, you could come up with a better line than that. Okay, I gotta give you credit. You are gorgeous but you are also arrogant, conceited and completely self-centred. You and I are going nowhere in a relationship."

I absolutely meant this with all my heart and soul. In retrospect, I wish I had heeded my own wise words. Somewhere along the line, though, I changed my mind. Incidentally, my best friend Paul hated Gary from the moment he met him. Paul bluntly told me that if I got involved with Gary, he would absolutely remove himself from my life. I never imagined that Paul would follow through. Paul kept his word, though, and I didn't see him for twenty-seven years.

As our relationship progressed, Gary told me he would accept Phyllis, my illegitimate child, as his own. He even wrote to his mother and pretended that the child was his. I was thrilled and grateful that my child would have a loving father and that I hadn't given in to everyone around me who wanted me to give my precious little girl up for adoption. My dad still didn't know about her, and she still lived in a foster home where I was able to see her every weekend. Gary got to know her pretty well and he was always so good and kind to her. He bought her gifts and made her laugh every time we went to visit. I began to envision us all living together 'happily ever after' in a quaint little house surrounded by a white picket fence.

Gary didn't waste much time before he asked my father for my hand in marriage. Dad didn't say no but he strongly suggested we wait a while. Two weeks later, the Armed Forces ordered Gary to do a tour of duty in Germany for three years starting in December 1961, a mere two months away. I always wondered if Dad, who was an officer, had anything to do with Gary getting sent to Europe. Gary and I decided he would spend one year in Germany, save as much cash as he could and I would do the same in Canada, and he would come home on his Christmas holidays to get married and our little family would relocate to Germany for the rest of his overseas stint.

The wedding date was set for December 19, 1962. My dreams were coming true. Gary was coming home on holidays to marry me and I was convinced that I was the envy of every female who had ever seen him. He arrived three days before our wedding. I went to the airport to greet him accompanied by his best man, John, and my friend and maid of honour, Phyllis, after whom I had named my daughter.

We drove to the airport in John's car which was an Austin Mini, a very small car that could only hold four people. I was sitting in the back on the right-hand side. On the way to the airport, the car door begin to squeak. I grabbed the door, wondering what was wrong with it. It was a fortunate move on my part because at that precise moment, the door became detached from the hinges and I was left holding it for the rest of the trip. I hung on for dear life because I didn't want anything to delay us. After a whole year of waiting around for Gary and even longer being a weekend visitor to my daughter, I was anticipating being reunited with my man.

As soon as we got to the airport, John called a repair man to fix the door. By the time that was done, we three ran into the airport. Gary was just walking through Customs. He dropped his luggage, grabbed me, spun me around and kissed me passionately.

"In three days," he whispered in my ear, "I will finally make you my woman. You are going to see that you'll never want to refuse me. You will be my woman."

I smiled, but I felt terrified. I did not like the sound of that, even a tiny little bit. My heart raced and I became flushed. I broke out into a sweat.

"Check out your little bride, Gary," John said, laughing. "Does she ever look excited about your wedding night."

"Yes," Gary joyously replied, "I am finally going to have my little one under my spell and control."

They both had misunderstood my terror for lust. Looking at Gary, I realized 'I don't know this man. I don't want to marry him. I want to run.' Terror struck but I remained silent. I felt like the cage had just closed around me and within it I'd be a helpless sexual slave, getting penetrated and touched and fondled when I didn't feel like it.

I had refused to have sex before our marriage, and now I realized that Gary wanted to marry me to get me into bed, pure and simple. He was lusting after someone who absolutely hated the idea of sex. I only wanted to have sex for the purpose of making babies but I knew now that I would have to put up with sex for Gary's sake. I decided that I would have to learn to move around like a nymph, faking moans and pants and facial expressions of lust and satisfaction in order for Gary to finish and leave his prisoner alone.

I married Gary in December 1962, just a month before my twenty-first birthday. Two weeks after our marriage, Gary returned overseas.

Once I was married, I was deemed a fit mother by Children's Aid, and Phyllis was no longer considered illegitimate. I was finally able to have my rights as a mother without interference, though I had to wait a couple of months, until we left for Germany.

My father still didn't know that Phyllis existed so I had to leave her in the group home until we set sail to join Gary overseas. Then I picked her up, and Phyllis and I traveled together to Germany. I was never able to tell my father about her, and I really didn't have a concrete reason. Each day that passed without him knowing made me more embarrassed to tell him. Also, my mother had begged me not to tell him because she thought that he would blame her. Mom had only been sober for a few years and was still insecure and blaming herself.

I certainly worried about my own ability to be a mother. I didn't even know which end of a baby to diaper and now suddenly I had the responsibility of being both a mother and a wife. Oh. My. God! I felt overwhelmed, terrified and inadequate in all aspects. Meshomis's teachings had not prepared me for motherhood or wifehood. In my mind, I could hear him telling me to just pray for help, do the best I could and everything would be fine. I felt an ominous sense of impending failure, and that there was nothing I could do about it. I could only hope that I didn't end up damaging my precious child.

Many unknowns became realities soon after Phyllis and I moved to Germany. We moved into a small, two-room, cold-water flat on the second floor of a beautiful house with a big back yard where Phyllis could play. Our landlord and his wife lived on the first floor. The landlady was a very loving, kind, caring individual who took me under her wing. She taught me a lot about mothering.

As I suspected it would be, sex was a problem from the first day. I learned to play this role slyly, to get Gary to leave me alone, but I learned to tone it down too. If I played my role too well, Gary would be finished in about four minutes, which was fabulous but then thirty minutes later he'd be back for more, with his erect penis and tactless demeanour; demanding a repeat session. And I would be obliged to re-enact my Academy Award performance.

I learned that my husband had been a chronic alcoholic since he was nineteen years old. I also learned he became abusive when he drank too much. I learned this the first year we were together. He beat me often. The first time he hit me was on the first Mother's Day we spent together. It was May 1963 and I had just discovered I was pregnant with his child. I was suffering from severe morning sickness and I had locked the door to the washroom to have privacy. I was washing my face and hands after throwing up, when Gary knocked down the door, grabbed me and threw me across the room. I landed against the far wall. He looked at me with hatred in his eyes.

"Don't you ever lock any door on me again or you will severely pay for it," he stated in a calm cold voice. "You got that, you bitch? Get the hell out of my sight and make me something to eat."

I reached my hand out for him to help me up, whimpering in pain, and uttering how sorry I was for upsetting him. He grabbed me, yanked me up and shoved me into the kitchen yelling, "Get in there, bitch."

This was the first of many beatings throughout our marriage. I quickly learned to kowtow to his every wish because I was terrified he would turn his vengeance towards my daughter. Gary never displayed any loving emotions towards her. It was a good thing that Phyllis was such a beautiful child because Gary was proud to show her off, and he treated her well in public. He was basically aloof with her unless she misbehaved, and then he was very strict. She was only two, but she seemed to understand that she had to follow my lead and she did her best to stay in the background. Phyllis and I made the best of it, and we spent quiet times together going for nature walks, colouring and reading bedtime stories together.

The Christmas season was the worst time in our marriage. Gary believed it was a time when everyone should stay in a drunken state. I, on the other hand, believed it should be a time made special for children. I didn't like anything to do with the partying aspect of the season.

It was our first Christmas Day together, just three days after our first anniversary, and I had just given birth to our daughter, Brandi. The army ambulance returned me and our newborn from the Iserlohn British Military Hospital to our home to Werle, Germany. I was so proud to present our new child to her father. I was absolutely certain that now everything would be all right and that Gary, I and our two girls would be a happy family.

Brandi and I were greeted at the door by Gary and Phyllis, who both looked very festive and happy. He had cooked a magnificent Christmas dinner with all the trimmings and after our feast, he spent time with our new little bundle of joy. We had a wonderful afternoon and I felt reassured that our future was going to be wonderful too. Gary started drinking in the late afternoon. Around supper time, he sent me to the corner store to get some milk. I was gone for about twenty minutes and when I got back, Phyllis's little back was starting to turn blue because he had slapped her. I was angry and called him a few choice names.

"You have to make a choice," he replied loudly. "It is me and our baby or it is your bastard. When we get back to Canada, you can't have it both ways."

I was stunned. I didn't know what to do. In those days, divorce was frowned upon, there was no such thing as Mother's Allowance and my father still didn't know that Phyllis existed. I made a conscious decision to do everything humanly possible to please Gary so that he wouldn't become angry and hit Phyllis again. My plan didn't work fully. He transferred his physical abuse to me but verbally abused her on a daily basis. After a couple of months of abuse I realized that neither Phyllis nor I could cope with life the way it was. In desperation, I contacted a Pentecostal Church Organization in Quebec City by mail to help me.

They were quick to reply that they had a good Christian family willing to adopt Phyllis and that if I truly loved her, I would let her go. Our lives were a living nightmare but I still held on to the hope that things would get better once we got back to Canada. This was not in the cards. We returned to Canada in September 1964, and the Pentecostal family was waiting for us at the airport. I felt incredible pain as I handed my child over to them. I wouldn't sign any papers for three months. I wanted to be sure that she was happy and I was hoping against hope that Gary would change his attitude.

December 22 was my second wedding anniversary. Two years of hell had passed, with the only joy in my life being my children. The Pentecostal family told me that if I truly loved Phyllis, I would let her go to a good family. They also told me that Gary would probably end up molesting Phyllis because he had already beaten her and heaped verbal abuse upon her. They went on to say that I was doomed to eternity in hell because I wouldn't repent for my sins. I never understood their logic. My child was a gift from the Creator, not a sin. However, I finally relented and signed away my rights as a mother to Phyllis.

The pain of letting Phyllis go was excruciating. It was a horrendous day. That very evening, the telephone rang. It was Beverly, the young babysitter whom Gary had mistaken me for years before. She was now eighteen years old.

"Bobbi, you've got to help me out," she begged me. "I can't take it anymore." She sounded so distraught, I was frightened for her.

"Beverly, what's the matter? Of course I will help you."

Her next words sent a chill through my body. "Bobbi, I'm so sorry. I am so sorry for hurting you. You have always been there for me. You've got to do something to stop your husband from contacting me." I felt like a knife was plunged into my chest. She continued, "I don't want to see him anymore. I've been sleeping with him. I care for Gary, but I want to break up our relationship and he won't give up. I'm not cut out to date a married man."

Gary was watching television. I hung up the phone and gave him the message, as matter-of-factly as I could. With tear-filled eyes, I stated, "Gary, that was Beverly on the phone. I think you know what she told me. If you tell me it isn't true, I'll believe you." I needed for him to say it wasn't true. I desperately needed to hear his denial. It was too much for me to cope with, knowing that just a few hours earlier, I had signed a paper giving up my beloved oldest child.

"It's true, Bobbi," he calmly replied with no remorse or guilt in his voice. It was almost like he was proud of himself. He didn't seem bothered at all.

At that moment I put any loving, gentle and other positive feelings I had on ice. I shut down my feelings and positive emotions. I had reached my breaking point. I had had enough. I vowed never to let myself be hurt again. It didn't occur to me to leave Gary. I had been well told that marriage is for better or for worse. This was for worse. I became like a robot, doing what was expected of me, presenting a well-adjusted family home, but I refused to feel. My brain and emotions went on strike. I didn't give a damn how Gary treated me. I didn't care what he did or who he did it with. There were many acts of cruelty aimed to destroy my self-esteem and self-worth but I outwardly reacted to none of them if they involved Gary. The only love I permitted myself to feel was love for my daughter Brandi, and I revelled in her love for me.

Brandi was so beautiful. When she was first born, she looked very Native, except for her blue eyes. She had lots of black hair and her skin was a tanned colour. She soon went bald and stayed that way for a couple of years, then grew beautiful blonde curly hair while her eyes turned dark brown. She was always such a well-behaved child and enjoyed the simplest of things. She was very smart and quick to learn. She was talking English fluently by eighteen months old.

Around this time was the beginning of my love affair with prescription drugs. It was a slow but progressive romance. This was the sixties, the new age of miracle medications. Pills were given out easily by the doctors because they had no idea about addiction. I began by following the prescriptions as written, but as time went on my need to escape grew and I took more pills. I began to go to several different doctors and to different drugstores so nobody would catch on to what I was doing.

I was determined never to become an alcoholic like my mother, so I allowed myself only two drinks a day. But I swallowed them with a handful of Valium. In order to stay in a non-feeling state, I was soon taking sleeping pills as well. As time went on, I became very familiar with Placydl, Nembutal and Largactil, just to name a few. I was willing to take anything to keep me numb. I didn't want to feel. I didn't want to 'be.' The Creator was good to me during this horrific time because I was able to maintain a loving, caring relationship with my beautiful Brandi and was able to care for her. I suffered with the thought that she would die, because it seemed that whoever I loved, I lost. I absolutely adored her and could not turn off my feelings for her. I realize today that this saved my life.

For Gary, life continued on, business as usual. He was a hard worker and a very dependable employee. He projected a charming personality to his friends, family and co-workers. However, something triggered within him when he came in contact with me. Even though he claimed to love me and he certainly adored his daughter, he continued to cheat on me. In my mind, this meant that everything was my fault. How could it be anyone else? I came to believe that I wasn't worthy of respect or love and had to pay for my sin of having sex before marriage. Therefore I had to accept Gary's promiscuity as a punishment for my evil thoughts and deeds before my marriage. My feelings towards his cheating remained frozen for a long time, with the help of pharmaceutical drugs and marijuana.

On December 31, 1965, I came home from a New Year's Eve party at the Legion in Dryden to catch my husband in bed with my first cousin. She was supposed to be babysitting our child. I looked at her lying underneath my husband and said, "Lola, go back to the guest room. I am tired and want to sleep." Then I popped a few pills because in order to maintain any sanity level, I couldn't allow any feelings of pain to surface.

The next day, after my breakfast of a cocktail variety of drugs, Brandi accompanied me as I drove Lola home to her mother's house. I was contemplating whether or not to tell Aunt Marie that her daughter was sleeping with my husband. I left Gary at home, sweating it out.

While we were at Aunt Marie's house, Uncle Stinky dropped in to say hello. He stomped over to the living room couch, plunked himself down, and called out to my daughter to come over and sit on his knee. I reacted. It seemed like every negative feeling I had ever experienced rose up and came spewing hideously out of my mouth, "Don't you even think of coming anywhere near any of my children, you overgrown fat tub of shit!" I leaped off my chair and grabbed Brandi.

I truly had no idea why I said this. I didn't know what possessed me. I was scandalized and embarrassed with myself. At the time I had no memories of being abused by him. "Oh my goodness, please forgive me. I can't imagine what came over me. I must be overtired," I apologized.

Aunt Marie and Uncle Roy's jaws dropped with astonishment. They had never seen me so ill-behaved. I had always presented myself like a lady.

"Of course I will forgive you," Uncle Stinky answered condescendingly, "as long as you let me make friends with your daughter." He patted his knee, gesturing to Brandi to sit there.

"Didn't you hear me the first time, you fat fucking idiot?" I yelled out, still shocked at the anger raging through my very being. Stinky gave up after that. Many years later I was able to make sense of my atrocious behaviour. At the time, my brain was only beginning to process the abuse that I had endured as a child.

On New Year's Eve of 1967, instead of celebrating the beginning of Canada's Centennial year with his wife, Gary left me at home with Brandi while he went out carousing with the neighbour's wife. By this time in the relationship, Gary didn't even pretend to keep his cheating from me. During supper that evening he brazenly looked me in the eye and stated, "Tonight I am bringing in the New Year with Karen. You stay here where you belong and take care of my child. Don't even think of phoning her husband or you know what will happen to you when I get home."

His secret was safe with me. After putting Brandi to bed, I smoked a joint, had a couple of rum and cokes, watched the Centennial celebrations on television and then went to bed. I felt lonely, afraid, worthless and useless so I popped a couple of pills. I lay there for a while thinking about my three recent miscarriages. I begged the Creator for another baby. I decided that I would try to have another child and if I lost another baby, I would take it as a sign that God did make junk after all and I was proof. Eventually I fell asleep.

Determined to stick to my idea of having another child, I threw out all my drugs and contraceptive pills and made a resolution to become an absolute saint, never have an evil thought, learn to be a perfect wife, and get pregnant, which was my main goal. I resolved not to drink or take drugs during pregnancy. I went through heavy withdrawal from stopping all those drugs cold-turkey. This involved violent vomiting, shaking, sweating and a whole lot of praying. Drug withdrawal was made easier because I used up a terrific amount of energy having sex. I not only survived the withdrawal, I was pregnant within a few months.

In those days, we were not supposed to have sex during the last six weeks of pregnancy, so I cut my charming husband off in early December. The cheating began again within a week.

The following New Year's Eve, I caught my husband having sex with another one of my relatives. It was my aunt this time. We were hosting a New Year's Eve party. Gary had sent me to bed after everyone but my aunt had left. I was way overdue in delivering the baby that I had begged the Creator for, so I was happy to retire and dutifully did as he said. Around 4 a.m., I got up to use the bathroom and caught the two of them having sex on our sofa bed. I didn't permit any feelings to surface. I went back to bed without them even knowing I had seen them.

I had stopped medicating myself when I became pregnant and my stress level was overwhelming. I felt suicidal. I began believing that everyone would be better off if I was dead. I decided that after I gave birth, I would try to have one more child as soon as I could. I wanted the little one I was carrying to have a playmate because Brandi was four years older and would be starting school soon. If I still felt suicidal after that, I would decide my fate.

My son was born in January, quickly followed by another son eighteen months later. Brandi and my two little boys helped me to decide to get off drugs for good. This was the one good decision I made during that time.

We moved across Canada several times during my marriage. I believed that relocating would help erase the negative memories from my mind. I tried to convince myself that in the new place, things would be better. Meshomis had always said that when we screw up, we just pick ourselves up, dust ourselves off and keep going. I took his words literally. Four months after my oldest son was born, Gary left his job, at my request, because he had simply cheated too many times in the little town we lived in. I felt like I could no longer hold my head up. We stopped off in Quebec City for a couple of months and then wandered to St. John's, Newfoundland. We stayed with Gary's parents for a couple of months until we both got employment and could afford to rent our own place and pay for a live-in babysitter. The next thing I knew I was pregnant again but I continued to work until I was six months along. Gary wasn't drinking too much so my life seemed to finally be working reasonably well until a phone call one bright, sunny day. I wondered who it was. I really hadn't allowed myself to make any friends, due to uncertainty pertaining to my husband. I hesitated to answer it in case Gary had run up some bills that he hadn't told me about.

"Oui, comment je peux vous aider?" I answered uneasily, in my best Parisian French.

"My dearie," a polite though firm female voice responded, "I hope you speak English to me because I was just talking to your mom so I know you can!"

"Yeah, right," I sarcastically replied. "Of course you did. You know her so well, she is like a sister to you." The thought rushed into my head that my mother had meddled in my life and contacted AA here so they would try to recruit me into their program. To my surprise the lady answered in a calm, matter-of-fact voice.

"Well, if the truth be told, I have never met your mom but she sounds like a very loving, caring person who dearly loves you. She thought that maybe you could do with some friends who have similar problems to you. And, little Missy, before you interrupt me, let it be known that I am not a member of AA. I belong to Al-Anon which is a twelve step program for relatives and friends of alcoholics. I would like to give you my phone number in case some day you need a friend, and by the way my name is Jessie."

A little voice deep within me told me that I needed that number in a big way, so I quickly wrote down her name and number. Hesitant to respond to this persistent woman who could pile a large amount of words together without taking a breath, I was pondering what to say when she broke the silence.

"Bobbi, I really hope and pray you will call me. It is very difficult living with anyone who abuses alcohol. So much baggage comes along with the alcohol such as getting beat up, getting cheated on, etcetera etcetera. I know, honey, because I've been in your situation."

I decided that going to these meetings couldn't hurt me, and after that I became what I thought was a staunch Al-Anon member. I knew that Al-Anon was a self-help program based on protecting the individual's anonymity and so I felt free, for the first time, to tell my life story. I was careful to point out that I was not only the child of an alcoholic, but was also the wife of a very active drinker. I did not mention my own problems with alcohol and drugs. I bewailed my fate because I definitely wanted to be recognized as the most hard-done-by woman that ever lived. These Al-Anon ladies seemed to see through all of my self-denial, and they told me I needed to get rid of my resentments before I could even begin to make any progress on myself. I also needed to become assertive and stick to whatever decisions I made. That seemed easy enough to do, because I blamed Gary for everything.

Within an hour of returning home from the meeting, I phoned Jessie.

"Hey Jess," I gleefully reported. "I got rid of all my resentments."

"My goodness, dearie, you did that rather quickly. How did you do it?"

"Well now," I answered. "When I got home I told Gary he had to leave immediately because he was causing me to have resentments. I just repeated everything all you guys told me. He got so angry, he packed his bags and left for his mother's."

Very diplomatically, Jessie explained that maybe I hadn't totally grasped the lesson of the meeting and perhaps I could continue to share my experiences if I made it a habit to continue going to meetings. It didn't take me long to realize that I had misinterpreted 'getting rid of my resentments.' I reunited with my husband, shortly before my youngest son's birth. A few months later, Gary left me.

Quite some time was to pass before this wonderful program actually clicked for me. At the beginning, I was completely immersed in the victim role and my reason for going to these meetings was basically to qualify as the most persecuted woman of all time. I became a staunch Al-Anon member. Ironically, after my second son was born, I became a closet drinker. I figured I had the booze under control because I never drank when I was pregnant, and never drank more than two drinks in public. However, I would wait until Gary had passed out for the night and then I would drink everything he had left. The next day he would question where the booze had gone, and I would convince him that he had experienced a black-out and had drunk it all himself. As a matter of fact, looking back on it, I believe the Creator sent me to those Al-Anon ladies so they could develop more patience, tolerance and love. I am sure I tested them.

My husband left us the morning of December 22, our seventh wedding anniversary. He left us with no money, no food and no oil for the furnace. My youngest boy was six weeks old, my oldest boy was almost two, and Brandi had just turned six on December 20. Because I was nursing the baby, I had enough milk in my system to feed the two boys, but this didn't help Brandi. Fortunately, a church organization brought me some baskets of food so we all ate. We were living in a rundown section of town, in a building that had been condemned by the city. The only heat source was a wood stove for cooking. There were two fireplaces which we couldn't use because the chimney was crumbling. At least we had electricity. I tried to grateful for that.

On Christmas Eve, Gary returned just to cause trouble. He showed up, extremely drunk, in the late afternoon.

"You are nothing but a whore," he snarled at me as he walked in the door. He shouted drunkenly that he was sure I was cheating on him because I never had sex with him so I must be getting it elsewhere. He beat me severely and left me unconscious.

When I came to, Brandi was doing her best to tend to me. As I regained consciousness I heard her talking to me. "Mommy, Mommy, please wake up. Mommy, are you dead? Mommy, I love you."

I painfully gathered her in my arms and told her I was okay. What a traumatic experience for a little girl to have to endure. To this day, she remembers the fear she felt as she witnessed her father beating her mother. Gary returned home shortly after New Year's and acted as if he hadn't even left. He denied having beaten me.

During the day, I continued trying to be the best mother possible. However, inwardly I knew that I was out of control, filled with anger, hate and the need for revenge. Al-Anon taught me to look within and to work on myself. I didn't like what I saw. Alcohol was becoming very important to me. I knew I had to get off the Black Path of destruction and find my way back to the Red Path.

My priority was to be a good mother and I knew this was impossible if I stayed with Gary.

I remember the exact moment I knew that I was leaving that man for good. I was lying on the floor exercising and listening to the radio. A beautiful song came on. It was the "Desiderata." Some of the words were "Avoid loud and aggressive people ... You are a Child of the Universe and you have a right to be here." These were magical words for me. They gave me the serenity to accept what I couldn't change and the courage to change the things I could. I decided to move back home with my family for a while. I thought that, because my mother was involved in her Alcoholics Anonymous program, I would have no urge to drink if I hung out with her and her friends.

The next day while Gary was at work, I bravely packed up myself and my three kids, and as many clothes as possible, and we returned to Quebec to live with my parents while I tried to figure out what to do.

Chapter Ten

I still did not accept the fact that I had the illness of alcoholism. I simply knew that everything would be okay because the "Desiderata" had said the universe was unfolding as it should and that I had a right to be here. I sure knew that I needed an escape from my life's troubles once in a while.

I had a difficult relationship with Alcoholics Anonymous, stemming from my childhood. As a teen I had made a vow to never become an alcoholic. I thought a drunken woman was the most repulsive human being alive. At the beginning of Mom's sobriety, she had forced me to go to Alcoholics Anonymous meetings with her. I remember occasions when someone was receiving acknowledgement for reaching a certain point of sobriety. How I hated it. Upon arrival we were met by a bunch of smiling faces but all I noticed was everyone was so old. It was mostly a bunch of men with wrinkly faces, bushy eyebrows, faded blue eyes and huge red noses. As far as I was concerned, they looked like a gang of perverts. I would hang on to Mom for dear life.

"Mom, you don't belong here with these grubby old men," I would whisper. "Dad and I can help you stay sober. I'll be good and I will do anything you ask me."

"Be quiet," she would reply sternly, "and listen to the messages these people share. It will help you to learn about alcoholism."

I thought my mother would rather hang out with those old losers than with me, and I resented AA even more. I closed my mind to anything those old geezers would talk about, so I never learned anything about the human side of alcoholism, such as the pain, suffering and remorse. As time went on, there were more and more alcoholics hanging around my parents' home, all in various stages of the disease. Some had a year or two of sobriety, some had a couple of days and some were drunk as skunks. Dad was so grateful that Mom was maintaining her sobriety, it seemed like he invited anyone without a home to come and live with us until they got themselves straightened out. At night-time, they would spread their sleeping bags all over the living room floor resulting in wall-to-wall alcoholics. Even as a teenager, though, I couldn't help but realize that many of the alcoholics were very nice people and a lot of them were well educated; they had lost everything because of the booze. I also noticed that the sober ones sure drank a lot of coffee. I assumed that caffeine must be somehow related to alcoholism, so I vowed never to drink coffee, either.

As I got older, Mom quit forcing me to go to the meetings with her but there was always AA literature around the house. I liked to read, so as a teenager I had memorized the entire program of recovery. From an intellectual point of view, I knew the twelve steps of recovery. I knew the twelve traditions which maintained group unity. I studied any information I could get my hands on if it pertained to alcoholism just to make sure that it would never happen to me. Later on, I had been a regular at Al-Anon meetings. I had known as an established fact that I was far too intelligent, and too aware of what alcohol could do to an individual, to fall into the trap of alcoholism. Nor would I ever marry an alcoholic/abuser. And yet here I was, recovering from taking too many prescription drugs, wanting to drink, and married to an abusive alcoholic.

"Oh well," I reasoned to myself, "I won't have any temptation to drink if I move in with my parents. Their home is just a block away from the AA club room so there will always be sober alkies visiting Mom at her house. Not only that, I'll be able to stay sober because I know better than them."

It became apparent very quickly that there simply wasn't enough room for me, my three kids and my parents in one home. So I applied for and received Mother's Allowance from the government, which enabled me to rent a little house just across the street from my parents and even closer to the AA meeting place.

My children were happy and loved. We had a loving extended family, and I should have been happy. I was miserable. I wanted to drink. I wanted an escape. I wanted to forget the past even if just for a little while. So I became a 'closet drinker' which means I hid my drinking. I only imbibed at night after my kids were asleep. Instead of the booze helping me, I became obsessed with when I would be able to drink again. I had felt the same way when I was nursing my children; always waiting to be able to stop nursing so I could pick up the bottle again. I began going to AA meetings with one purpose in mind. I never said I was there for myself; I pretended to be there as my mother's guest. I thought that maybe there was something I had missed in the teachings and if I found it, I wouldn't want to drink anymore. Needless to say, that plan of action didn't work so my next goal was to make the members dislike me to the point of rejection. My logic was if I could manage to get myself kicked out of Alcoholics Anonymous, I could drink in peace and would be able to blame the fellowship. What a great excuse it would be. I could hear myself saying to my friends, 'I thought I should stop drinking and I even went to AA but they kicked me out. I guess they realized I didn't qualify as a member.'

I went to the meetings and criticized everyone. I would say horrible things like, "You are a bunch of weak-willed sons-of-bitches that should be lined up and shot. Here you are, at these stupid meetings, and you don't even care what's happening with your spouse and kids."

Their response was always, "Keep coming back, Bobbi, and never forget that we love you."

My efforts totally backfired. After a few months of banging my head against the wall, closet drinking, and trying to get kicked out, I finally gave up and said out loud to myself, "Bobbi, you are an alcoholic. Quit trying to beat the system. It ain't gonna work."

A non-alcoholic would never have behaved in such an idiotic fashion. I certainly wasn't happy with this self revelation. I came into the fellowship of recovery kicking and screaming all the way. I felt angry and resentful, like all the work I had put into making sure I would never develop this illness had been a waste of time.

My logic told me that if I admitted to having this disease the Creator would reward me by making the rest of my life a bed of roses. I figured if I stopped drinking and tried to be the best mother ever born, the powers that be would send me only positive stuff to deal with. Not for one moment did it occur to me that having a good life would require an attitude adjustment on my part.

I wondered whether other people were convinced their lives would unfold a certain way just to find out that there was some other power that could and would change all their plans. Eventually I learned that living your life on a four-lane highway, full speed ahead, is somewhat dangerous and certainly risky. Why hadn't I seen that before? Anybody but a fool would know that it is better to walk slowly and peacefully along a path, thinking things through before making decisions.

I had instead jumped on a merry-go-round that had spun out of control. A merry-go-round named denial. I had been denying there was a power greater than me in the world. Many times I found myself at odds as to what to do. I imagined all kinds of ways my plan could be sabotaged. In other words, I worried myself sick over how my plan might not work. At the same time, I had the nerve to tell people that I believed in God (or the Creator of All Things). I told people that He was a God of love and that He loved us all and would take care of us all.

In actuality, I didn't believe that at all. If I had, I would have stopped trying to get the Creator to do things my way. Looking back, I firmly believed this power greater than myself needed me as His supervisor. Who in the hell did I think I was? I had the unbelievable gall to question the Creator's will. I could twist things around so that circumstances looked like they were anybody else's responsibility other than mine. I knew how to play the victim role to perfection and oh how I played it. I loved blaming my mother for everything and I fed my resentment towards her every day.

For sixteen months, while I tried to muddle through the twelve steps of recover, I binge drank. No wonder I didn't make much progress. The problem was, I was attacking the program with a vengeance from an intellectual viewpoint. I refused to accept the Higher Power concept of Alcoholics Anonymous, the spiritual component of the program. I wrongfully confused 'spiritual' with 'religious.' I should have known differently, because Meshomis had taught me better.

At this point I was attending AA meetings regularly, and had managed to be sober for a few months. I was doing what is called the third step and searching for the 'right' spiritual foundation. I was trying to decide who was the right God to believe in, so I decided to join every church denomination in my area to make sure I got the right one. One church practiced being completely dunked into water by the minister. It was not like a Catholic baptism where the priest douses you with a little bit of holy water. No. This church put you in water from head to toe, like John the Baptist did. I figured this would get me in God's good graces. The night of the baptism, I was dressed in jeans and a bright red cotton top. I was sure that I looked classy and chic, but in retrospect I must've looked a little too sexy for my Baptism. The minister told me that I looked sleazy.

"Oh well," I said, "you can pray for me and everything will be fine." I thought that was a classy response.

The congregation, the minister and I all went to a medium-sized indoor pool in a high-class hotel—a classic baptism setting. The pool smelled of chlorine. Each member of the congregation had brought lawn chairs which they placed all around the pool.

The minister and I got into the water while the congregation stood between the chairs and the pool holding hands forming a closed circle around the pool. They all closed their eyes. While I took in this foolish-looking scene, the congregation began to chant "Praise the Lord, save this sinner" over and over again. I thought to myself that they looked like they needed saving a lot more than me. They looked totally ridiculous. The minister stood to my side, put one hand on my back, the other on my forehead. He then proceeded to trip me by kicking my foot out from under me and shoved and held me under water. He immediately pulled me back out of the water, spitting and sputtering and trying to catch my breath.

"Are you saved?" the minister yelled out.

"No, I don't think so," I replied.

Down I went again. This time, for longer. When I was brought up, he asked again if I was saved. I thought of lying and saying that

I was, but I remembered Meshomis telling me the importance of being honest.

"No," I said. "Not yet!"

He shoved me under water for the third time, and I thought, 'This just ain't gonna happen again! Strike three and you're out! If I don't tell them I'm saved they're going to think I'm possessed or something.'

"Are you saved?" the preacher asked for the third time.

I mustered up a pious, saintly look and I yelled at the top of my lungs, "Yes! I am saved! Jesus loves me! Praise the Lord! Hallelujah!"

I would have said anything to get out of there. I rubbed my eyes clear of water and glanced all around me. The congregation was sitting on their lawn chairs chanting in unison, "Praise the Lord, we have witnessed a miracle." I quickly got out of the pool, got changed and went home. I didn't stay for the reception afterwards. I wasn't going to spend any more time with those weirdos. No thanks.

'It will be another miracle if those idiots ever see me again,' I thought. 'I ain't going there no more! It just ain't gonna happen!' I was also thinking, 'So much for Meshomis's theory of being honest.' Honesty could kill if you let it go on too long.

I had good intentions. I had joined several different churches to beat the odds and get into heaven. My thought process was if I joined all of the churches, God would take kindly to me and I'd never have to eat worms again. But nothing happened. Nothing. I prayed and I prayed and I prayed and I prayed—but nothing happened. Even after all that praying, nothing happened until I finally relinquished control.

I had by now managed to be sober for sixteen months. I succumbed for one evening, which happened to be on Christmas, with a few hours of binge drinking. I blacked out after a few drinks. After my binge, I felt so awful I fell to my knees in despair and complete surrender. I looked up to the sky and genuinely and humbly begged, "Creator, please help me." This was the first time I had said it and actually meant it.

He did. He responded almost immediately by leading me back to Meshomis. Shortly after my one-day drunk, I received news that my grandfather was in the hospital with emphysema. I knew

I had to go to him immediately. I needed to tell him how much I loved him and how much he had taught me. My parents paid my train fare and volunteered to look after my kids while I was gone, so I wasn't on any kind of a time limit. I took the two-day train trip back to the little community in Northern Ontario. I prayed to be given the appropriate words to tell him how I felt about him. I was well known in the family for not being particularly diplomatic, and usually sticking my foot in my mouth. I wanted to show him what a cool, calm and collected individual I had become. I was still in my manipulative, denial mode but that was soon to change.

I arrived at the hospital with a sense of anticipation at seeing this wonderful old man whom I hadn't seen in three years. However, as I walked down the hall to his room, my body filled with feelings of guilt, remorse and shame for not having listened to the words of wisdom that he had always been so willing to share with me. As I opened the door to his room, I heard a loud guffaw followed by his joyful voice.

"Come in, come in, my precious little twerp. I have missed you and am so pleased that you have come to say goodbye."

I thought that was a strange thing to say. I hadn't even had time to say hello and he was thinking that I was saying goodbye. How weird was that.

"I know you remember my offerings of tobacco to the Creator whenever we were going to have a talk," Meshomis continued. "I need you to do that for me now because I am not well enough to go outside. Please put the tobacco over by the cedar tree and then bring me a small piece of the cedar for my room. Don't forget to thank the Creator for all the good things that have happened in our life and thank the tree for giving us a branch to use to protect me as I leave this world."

None of these words were what I expected to hear. Deep down inside, though, I knew that it was necessary to do exactly as he said, so I quickly completed these tasks. When I returned to the room, Meshomis took a little rock out of his Medicine Pouch.

"Angekwe, this little rock has travelled with me for many years now. It is very special to me and I want to pass it on to you with my Medicine Pouch. Always treat everything that comes from Mother

Earth with honour and respect. Come and hold my hand while I talk."

He gently placed the rock back in the Medicine Pouch and hung it around my neck.

"My precious one, it is time for me to go to the Spirit World," he said. "I know you will feel sadness but remember that you will be feeling sad for yourself just because I will not be visible to you anymore. I will always be your Spirit Guide. I want you to feel joy for both you and me. I want you to celebrate the great love we have shared all your life. I know that as a grandfather, I wasn't supposed to have favourite grandchildren, but you know as well as I do that you were always my number one. I didn't see you often but the bond was unbroken.

"Thank you for sharing your life with me and I thank you for your clean and sober life. I am so proud of you. I have one last thing for you to do. When you leave here and you are feeling weak, take the rock out of the pouch, put it in your hand and keep rubbing it until you feel better. It will give you the strength you need. Today when you are gone from me, I want you to spend some time alone and ask the Spirits for words of gratitude to express your rock's strength, and use those words as a prayer always. I want to say goodbye now. In the Indian way, the only time we say goodbye is when one is leaving for the Spirit World."

I gave this wonderful man a kiss on his forehead. I told him that I would do everything I could to honour him and the Creator for the rest of my life. I turned around and left the room knowing that I would never see him again. And I was okay with that. I knew Meshomis was looking forward to being with the Creator.

The next day I returned to Quebec knowing that as soon as possible my children and I would be coming back to this area to live a peaceful, loving and sober life. Oh, I knew it wouldn't be easy but it could be done.

Armed with an inner peace and strength that I had never before experienced, I was able to file for divorce and move back to my Ojibwa roots in Northern Ontario and raise my children to the best of my ability in a sober and fairly sane way.

After the divorce, I was able to enjoy Christmas a lot more than before. I could gather my children around me on the couch and read Bible stories and Indian legends to them. It was important to me that my children knew about the spiritual values of both White and Native cultures. I told them the legend about the prophet that came to our country and gave us many teachings and prophecies about what had been, what was coming and what would be. As my children grew, their friends would all come over on Christmas. These were happy times with much laughter and love shared all around.

My oldest daughter, Phyllis, tracked me down by telephone when she was almost eighteen years old. She told me that her adoptive father had sexually abused her from the time she was six. This was horrific news to hear on our first contact. I was deliriously happy to hear from her though and sent money for her to come and join us. She arrived the following week. I went to the airport to meet her with a psychologist friend of mine. My friend wanted to see how we would interact after such a long separation, and I was happy to have someone there to be my support. I was afraid—terrified actually. I didn't know what would be appropriate to say or to do. I was scared of my reaction. There wasn't much airport security so I was able to be right at the window waiting for her. Even though I hadn't seen her since she was four years old, I recognized her the moment she got off the plane. I said, "That's her." I just knew, even though she didn't look like me or any of her half-siblings. Nor did she look like her father. She was as cute as a button, standing all of five foot one and weighing about one hundred pounds.

Phyllis seemed genuinely pleased to find me. We went home and told my other children, who were eight, ten and fourteen years old at the time, about who she was. They were amazed to find out they had another sister and accepted her immediately.

Within days, everything changed. I found out she had nothing but contempt and hatred for me. She blamed me for everything miserable in her life. One Sunday evening just after supper, she and her siblings were in the living room watching television. I was having a cup of tea feeling content that all my children were together when she suddenly appeared in the kitchen and began screaming all of her pent-up hatred at me.

"Bobbi, I am going to get even with you for giving me up. If you hadn't copped out on me, I would never have been raped by my adoptive father. When I have children you will never see them."

I was stunned into silence. I didn't know what to say or do. I looked over at my other children, who had followed her into the kitchen. My youngest son straightened his shoulders, trying to appear bigger than he was. He jutted out his chin and announced, "You quit being rude to my mommy right now. I don't like you anymore." My older son joined his brother and stood beside him. My younger daughter, Brandi, came and stood beside me. I didn't know what to answer Phyllis. At that moment, I thought she was right. I was no good.

"Phyllis." I stood up and looked her in the eye. "Not a day has gone by that I didn't think of you. I did what I thought was right at the time. I am so very sorry for what happened to you but am so happy that you found us at last. I hope we can be a family."

She did not accept this response and left my home that night. She basically kept her word, and I never saw her children. I say basically because I saw her oldest child, my oldest grandson, when he was eighteen months old and again when he was eighteen years old. I have never seen her other two boys, but I hope one day I will.

Once my other kids grew up and left home I moved back to Quebec City to be close to my parents. Now I enjoy the holidays, sharing time with my beloved parents and all my sober friends and acquaintances.

Gary went on to marry again and had three more sons. After twenty-five years of marriage, he and his second wife divorced. Gary's wife had refused to allow him to associate with me in any way, including with the grandchildren. She was jealous of me. I never quite understood why because she is the one he left me for. Last year, while visiting my two sons who now live in Edmonton, Alberta with their families, I saw my ex-husband and was finally able to come to terms with him and spend some quality time. For the first time we were able to spend time with the grandchildren together as grandparents.

Gary made amends for the way he treated me and complimented the way I had brought up the children. "Bobbi, you are a great mother," he said. "Our children have turned out to be responsible, stable adults with a good education. They are considerate spouses and great parents. This is all thanks to you. I can take no credit for any of it."

Instead of gloating, I looked at this poor broken man and my heart filled with compassion for him. He is still an active alcoholic and my first thought was the old cliché, 'There but for the grace of God, go I.' He looks upon himself as a failure and is despondent most of the time, finding solace only with our children. His three other sons live with him but show him no respect and have no use for him.

We parted as friends and now keep in touch occasionally by telephone. I encourage him, to the best of my ability, to concentrate on his good qualities. Unfortunately, he seems unable to forgive himself. Fortunately, I realize that I can't fix him. He has to deal with his own demons.

My old friend Paul and I reunited after I moved back to Quebec City. It was really strange how I tracked him down. I had been looking for him for years to no avail and had basically given up on ever seeing my best friend again when I ran into his younger brother, Peter, at an AA meeting. He was a newcomer to sobriety and was glad to see a friendly face.

"Hey, Bobbi, remember me?" He latched on to me immediately, speed-talking. "I'm Paul's brother. I hope you remember me 'cause I sure don't feel comfortable with all these strangers. My God, I haven't seen you in years. Paul was telling me he would love to see you again but he has no idea where you live."

My whole body just froze. I couldn't speak, I couldn't think, I couldn't move. I couldn't believe my ears. Paul wanted to see me again. He had forgiven me for marrying Gary. Hallelujah! After my senses returned, I was able to get details about Paul. I phoned him right after the meeting. We recognized each others' voices immediately. We made arrangements for him to come to Quebec City the following week for a short visit. All these years he had lived only about five hundred miles away from Quebec City. It was a beautiful reunion and we got to spend a few days together getting caught up on each other's lives. Not having had any siblings of my own, I never really understood my feelings for this wonderful man. I now realize that our feelings for each other could perhaps be similar to the way twins feel about each other. We kept in touch by phone after that. Unfortunately, Paul developed Alzheimer's but we remained good friends until his death last year.

My mom has become my best friend and is still active in Alcoholics Anonymous. We have learned to accept each other as we are now, and have become very close. Mom has maintained a sober life since 1956 and has been an inspiration to thousands of others. Most of all, she has shared unconditional love with everyone she knows, and she was instrumental in my maintaining sobriety.

I credit Ookashahgumme-kwe for teaching me the destruction I would face if I didn't turn my life around. Meshomis taught me that I have a gift of being able to choose how I command my will. I can choose the Black Path or the Red Path. I have chosen the Spiritual way of life and do my best to stay on the Red Path. Whenever things get really rough I take the rock out of my Medicine Pouch, place it in my hand, gently rub it with my thumb and say:

> Thank you, precious rock for showing yourself to me and giving me permission to use you to gather strength in all ways.
> Drained physically with the unnecessary burdens I have been carrying for so long;
> Drained mentally because of having such a short-term memory;
> Drained emotionally because of fears of not being able to finish what I know I must do;
> Drained spiritually as I fought sharing the teachings I had been given.
> As I pick you up and look at you, I feel re-energized when I see how you have been treated and you are still here.
> The scars that you have developed because of being

kicked around and disrespected, not unlike us humans, jump out at me.

As I hold you close to my heart and look at you once again, I see how you turned those scars around.

With vivid clarity I witness a gleeful smile appear on your face.

I turn you over and see the smoothness interrupted by the imprint of an eagle soaring high, taking our prayers to the Creator.

I know now that you will live in my Reclaiming bundle to remind me to nurture myself in the right way to keep my strength balanced and I will call you 'Migisi.'

It is a wonderful feeling to know you are not alone, that no matter what colour your skin is, no matter what your beliefs are, there is a Supreme Being watching over you, guiding you, loving you. That you are not junk. I know this to be true because God Don't Make No Junk.